How to
Build
Wealth
with your
401(k)

EVERYTHING YOU NEED

TO KNOW TO BECOME

MORE THAN A MILLIONAIRE

OVER THE COURSE OF

YOUR WORKING LIFETIME.

Steve Merritt, MBA
SECOND EDITION

Halyard Press
Melbourne, Florida

This publication is designed to provide accurate and authoritative information in regard to the subject matter covered. It is sold with the understanding that neither the author nor the publisher is engaged in rendering legal, accounting, or other professional service. If legal advice or other expert assistance is required, the services of a competent professional person should be sought.
From a Declaration of Principles jointly adopted by a Committee of the American Bar Association and a Committee of Publishers.

© 1997 by Steve Merritt
first edition copyrighted in 1995

Published by:
Halyard Press, Inc.
P.O. Box 410308
Melbourne, FL 32941-0308
800-791-2111; Fax: (407) 636-5370.

Printed in the United States of America

Publisher's Cataloging-in-Publication
(Prepared by Quality Books, Inc.)
Merritt, Steve.
    How to build wealth with your 401(k) : everything you need to know to become more than a millionaire over the course of your working lifetime / Steve Merritt. --2nd ed.
    p. cm.
    ISBN 1-88706-304-8

    1. 401(k) plans. 2. Finance, Personal. 3. Retirement--Planning.
4. Individual retirement accounts--United States. I. Title.

HG179.M47 1997   332.024'01
                           QBI97-40203

Dedication

To Sandy, my wife, best friend and partner. She took my
vision and transformed it into a tangible asset that has
helped thousands of people and will continue to benefit
thousands more.

Table of Contents

List of Tables

List of Figures

Note to the Reader

This book is written for you, and others just like you, who have been given full responsibility for managing your 401(k) account but have been given very little instruction on how to do it. With a 401(k), there is no trained fund manager investing your money and investment results are not guaranteed. The final value of your account is almost entirely determined by the choices you make along the way. If you know what you're doing, you can use your 401(k) to amass large amounts of money over the course of your lifetime. It is entirely possible to create a $1 million nest egg if you start early and make good investment decisions.

To make this happen, you need the right information. While there are perhaps hundreds of books available on investing, this one specifically addresses your needs as a 401(k) investor. It is based on my knowledge as a corporate 401(k) investment advisor and on my experience as an investment educator working with people like yourself. I can help you because I am a 401(k) investor myself.

Most books tend to gloss over subjects with general information. "How to Build Wealth with your 401(k)" is different. The pages that follow are packed with details and step-by-step instructions. You will come away with several tools that can immediately be applied to improve the performance of your investments. You will learn exactly how to analyze each investment in your plan and determine which are good and which are bad. I will show you how stocks, bonds and cash equivalents work from a practical approach. For example, you will learn why bond funds can produce negative returns and that stocks occasionally have negative returns but they outperform fixed income investments over a long period of time.

The material in this book is for participants in 401(k) and similar plans (i.e. 403(b), 457, Thrift Savings Plan for federal employees, SIMPLE, and SAR-SEP plans). Beginning investors can jump right in and get started. Experienced investors will find material they haven't seen anywhere else. There is more information packed into this book than in a dozen others. So, turn the page and get started. The rewards are out there waiting for you!

Chapter 1

Sources of Retirement Income

In order to achieve life satisfaction and financial success at retirement, you must take specific actions as early as possible. The first step is to decide what type of life you want to enjoy at retirement so you can estimate your income needs. Table 1.1 gives an example of the amount you may need based on your current income.

In the past, retirees were a small, inactive group with modest means and a short life span. Retirees are now living longer and are an active segment of our society. Today, we can expect to live an average 20 years after retirement. Where will the money come from to support us during this time of our life? The three major income sources are Social Security, personal savings, and company retirement plans. Let's look at each in turn.

Social Security

The Social Security Act of 1935 mandated a government controlled and administered pension plan. The plan was started to help supplement the personal savings of retired workers. It was not (and is not) designed to meet all your financial needs during retirement. It is intended solely to supplement other income sources. In fact, Social Security will only replace, on average, about 20 to 40 percent of your income. The program is funded by FICA (Federal Insurance Contributions Act)

Table 1.1   Savings Needed At Retirement

Years to Retirement	Present Income	Savings Needed at Retirement
0	$30,000	$96,400
	$40,000	$200,712
	$50,000	$312,191
	$60,000	$432,669
10	$30,000	$106,280
	$40,000	$247,710
	$50,000	$396,354
	$60,000	$563,220
20	$30,000	$95,263
	$40,000	$287,783
	$50,000	$482,012
	$60,000	$712,979

This is an estimate of the amount of money you will need for retirement in addition to Social Security. It assumes that you will need 80 percent of your current income.

taxes. You and your employer must both pay 7.65 percent of your gross wages towards FICA taxes. A total of 15.3 percent is contributed on your behalf. Contributions to Social Security are mandatory. You must participate.

Personal Savings

There are many types of personal savings. A few examples may be: equity in your principle residence, a second home, rental property, Investments, and Individual Retirement Arrangements (IRA).

Traditional Company Retirement Plans

There are no requirements for an employer to provide a retirement plan. They are set up voluntarily. If a company does choose to provide a qualified plan, then certain guidelines must be met. These guidelines are imposed by the Department Of Labor and the Internal Revenue Service. There are two categories of employer provided retirement plans: defined benefit and defined contribution. *Defined benefit* plans are the traditional company pension plan. They pay a fixed dollar amount to employees after retirement. The payout is typically based on a formula involving years of service and salary. Financing, investing and administration are all handled by the employer.

Today's Retirement Plans

Extensive government regulations and soaring expenses have forced companies away from traditional pensions. Today, more companies are choosing *defined contribution* plans. Many pension plans have been replaced with defined contribution plans over the past ten years. Experts believe that the traditional company pension will disappear by the next century.

In a defined contribution plan, the employer generally makes periodic payments into the employee's retirement fund. A qualified salary reduction plan allows employees to save part of their earnings on a tax-deferred basis. A defined contribution plan is different from a defined benefit in several ways. First, the amount of money going into the account is known but the money paid out is not known until the employee retires. The final amount depends on how successfully the funds were invested. Second, the company does not have to make contributions. If it does, it may elect to stop or change the amount at any time.

Money Purchase Plan

The money purchase plan is a hybrid between contribution and pension plans. Contributions are mandatory. The benefit is dependent on final account value which is a result of how well the investment did over the years. This is not a very popular plan.

Profit Sharing Plan

In a profit sharing plan employers make contributions based on profits. The first known profit sharing plans were established about 100 years ago by Pillsbury Mills and Procter & Gamble. The profit sharing plan is one of the most popular defined contribution plans. It comes in different packages and is the basis for all defined contribution plans.

Savings or Thrift Plan

This type of retirement plan was set up to encourage employees to save. Employee contributions may be after-tax and employer's contributions may be pre-tax.

Employee Stock Ownership Plan

The Employee Stock Ownership Plan (ESOP) was set up to allow investments in the employer's company stock. This is basically a profit sharing plan that invests only in company stock.

401(k) Plan

The original defined contribution plans dated back as long as 100 years ago and were funded by employer contributions. These companies gave employees the option to receive a portion of their salary or bonuses in cash or to defer it on a tax-deferred basis into an investment plan. The arrangement was called a Cash or Deferred Arrangement (CODA). It was not formally recognized under tax code until the Revenue Act of 1978. The Internal Revenue Code was amended to add section 401(k) which allows private sector employees to contribute part of their salary on a tax-deferred basis into a qualified retirement plan. This is a voluntary arrangement - employers do not have to offer it. The 401(k) plan (named after section 401(k) in the

IRC) was born. It is the foundation of all employee salary deferred retirement plans such as the 403(b), 457, and Federal TSP.

As a defined-contribution savings plan, the 401(k) allows private sector employees to divert a portion of their salary into a tax-sheltered savings account where it accumulates tax-free. Employees make selections from investment options made available by the employer. Some employers match up to 100 percent of the employee's contribution. This is an easy way to double your money. Its just like giving yourself a raise.

The 401(k) has become one of the most popular retirement savings plans because it is inexpensive to run. It has also become one of the most powerful retirement vehicles because it gives the middle class the opportunity to become millionaires over the course of their working lifetime. Here are six reasons why your 401(k) is the best investment you can make.

(1)   **Tax Breaks** The contributions you make toward your 401(k) reduce your taxable income. You do not pay federal or state income taxes on this money. Of course you are only deferring your taxes. Uncle Sam still wants his share and it is due when you begin using the money at retirement.

(2)   **Employer Match** Some employers make matching contributions to your account. This is just like getting a raise.

(3)   **Access to the Money** All 401(k) plans allow hardship withdrawals, but many also allow you to borrow money from your savings in the form of a loan. The interest from your loan goes back into your account.

(4)   **Portability** When you change jobs, you can transfer your money into an IRA, or in many cases, transfer it to your new 401(k) plan.

(5)   **Convenience** Your contribution is automatically taken out of your paycheck. You don't even have to write a check and the paperwork is minimal. Your employer sends you a statement and you file it.

(6)   **Control** Another advantage of your 401(k) is control. You get to decide which investment is best for you. Of course you should also keep in mind that if you blow it, there is no government agency to bail you out at the end.

While the final payout of your 401(k) cannot be determined in advance, you have the opportunity to receive more than what Social Security and company pensions combined could provide. But there's a catch. Your funds must be invested wisely or you may end up very disappointed when you retire.

403(b) Plan

The 403(b) plan is a qualified salary deferral retirement plan for employees of certain nonprofit and tax-exempt organizations. It is a common plan among public schools and churches. Investment principles in a 403(b) (how to invest your money) are similar to those of the 401(k) although plan mechanics (loans, contribution levels, etc.) may be a little different. New legislation enacted in 1997 brings 403(b) salary reduction agreements under the same rules as those governing 401(k) plans. Employees can now defer up to $9,500 of their salary into a 403(b) plan. This amount is indexed to inflation so it will increase periodically as needed. Many 403(b) plans are structured as a variable annuity. Be sure to read Appendix C if you have a 403(b) and it is set up this way.

457 Plan

The 457 is a retirement plan created for state and municipal entities in which participants contribute money and make investment decisions. Historically, 457 plans have had the least favorable features of all the salary deferral plans. For example, the maximum contribution level was limited to $7,500 with no indexing for inflation. The money in a 457 plan was considered an asset of the company. This left retirement funds vulnerable to bankruptcy claims and non-retirement uses by the employer. Legislation enacted in 1997 has significantly improved the 457 plan. The maximum contribution level in 1997 is still $7,500 but it is now indexed to inflation and the funds are no longer considered assets of the company. Investment assets are now held in a trust and kept separate from general corporate assets.

Federal Thrift Savings Plan

The Thrift Savings Plan (TSP) is a retirement plan for federal employees. It is very similar to the 401(k) and offers matching contributions, index funds and low expense to plan participants. It is an excellent defined contribution plan.

Keogh, SEP, SAR-SEP, and SIMPLE

The Keogh, Simplified Employee Pension (SEP), Salary Reduction Simplified Employee Pension (SAR-SEP) and Savings Incentive Match Plan (SIMPLE) are all retirement plans created for small businesses and self-employed individuals. The SEP and SIMPLE allow salary deferral. They operate similar to the IRA but allow larger contributions.

Individual Retirement Account (IRA)

The IRA is a retirement plan that is available to anyone with earned income. It is not associated with your employer. You can invest in an IRA even if you participate in a company retirement plan. Your contributions may be tax-deductible depending on your income level and eligibility to participate in your employers retirement plan. The IRA is an excellent complement to your company retirement plan and should not be overlooked.

Times Have Changed

If you have a traditional defined benefit pension, you can expect a moderate payout when you retire without ever having to get involved in investment decisions. Today, most people have some type of defined contribution plan such as the 401(k), 403(b), 457, and Federal TSP, where there is no longer a trained pension fund manager taking care of your retirement account. While your employer is responsible for selecting the investment options, it is your responsibility to choose what percentage of money to put into each of the available funds. The final value of your account is determined by how well you make these decisions. This is why it's important for you to learn how your 401(k) works and how to make informed investment decisions. Let's get started.

Chapter 2

Get to Know Your 401(k) Plan

How Your 401(k) Makes Money

The 401(k) as an investment vehicle has two advantages that give it more leverage than other investments: tax breaks and employer contributions. You can get thousands of dollars more to your account by starting early, contributing often, and investing wisely.

Tax Breaks

The contributions you make toward your 401(k) reduce your taxable income. You do not pay federal or state income taxes on this money until you retire. This is called tax deferment. You get immediate tax savings and leverage in the growth of your investment because you have more money to invest. Here's a second tax advantage - not only is your *contribution* tax-deferred but your investment *grows* tax-deferred. Now your money can really grow. Let's look at an example.

Let's say you invest $3,000 a year for 40 years and earn 10 percent. If you pay 28 percent in taxes on this money, you will only have $2,160 left over to invest. Your final balance in this case will be $486,768. If you defer taxes on this investment, you can get the full $3,000 to work for you and your balance will be an incredible $1,460,555. You end up with $973,787 more thanks to tax deferral! See Figure 2.1.

Figure 2.1   Advantage Of A Tax-Favored Investment

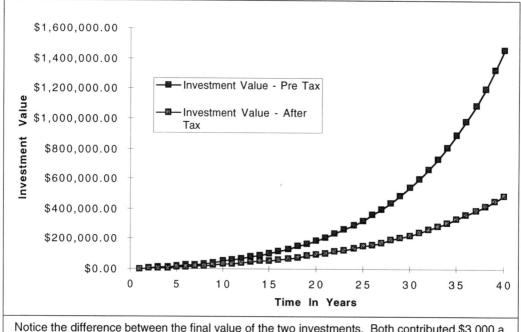

Notice the difference between the final value of the two investments. Both contributed $3,000 a year with a 10 percent return. The investment with the greatest value was tax-deferred.

Here's another way to look at it. If you are in the 28 percent tax bracket, you will save $280 for every $1,000 you contribute to your 401(k). As your investment grows tax-free, Uncle Sam is effectively matching 28 percent towards your retirement. Deferring taxes will allow you to triple the amount of money you can accumulate. Take a look at Table 2.1 to see what tax deferral means to your bottom line. Although you are not paying federal and state income taxes on your contributions, you are still required to pay FICA on the full amount of your gross income.

Employer Match

Your employer may match your contribution. Think of this match as "free" money. Suppose you contribute $1,800 a year for 40 years and your investment earns 10 percent. Without an employer match, your investment will be worth $876,333. In contrast, if your employer matches 50 percent, your investment will be worth $1,314,500! This is a difference of $438,166!

   How To Build Wealth With Your 401(k)

Table 2.1 Impact Of A Tax-Favored Investment On Your Bottom Line

	Case 1 no tax deferral	Case 2 with tax deferral	difference
Gross earnings	$40,000	$40,000	N/A
Impact of deferred contribution			
Deferred contribution (6% of gross earnings)	N/A	$2,400	N/A
Taxable earnings	N/A	$37,600	N/A
Taxes on earnings at 28%	N/A	$10,528	$(10,528)
After-tax earnings			
Net pay (minus taxes and deferred contributions)	$40,000	$27,072	$12,928
Net paycheck	$769	$ 521	$249
Total annual compensation (gross earnings minus taxes)	$40,000	$29,472	$10,528

Your compensation is 1.7 percent greater in Case 2 where 6 percent of your earnings is tax-deferred. Even though your paycheck is $33.23 smaller in Case 2, your total compensation is greater thanks to tax savings. Total Annual Compensation is equal to Gross Earnings minus taxes.

Even though your employer's contribution totaled $36,000, you end up with an additional $438,166! See Figure 2.2. If your employer matches 100 percent instead of 50 percent, you end up with $1,752,666. Not bad for an investment that many people don't even bother to take advantage of!

Rule 1: Start Early

Retirement planning is the classic "Catch 22". The closer you are to retirement, the easier it is to estimate your income needs but the harder it is to accumulate the money. The farther away you are the harder it is to estimate your income needs, but the easier it is to accumulate the money. Let's use Ben and Jerry as an example. Both are young men of 25 (who love ice cream). They intend to continue working 40 years until the age of 65.

Figure 2.2   Matched vs. Unmatched Contributions

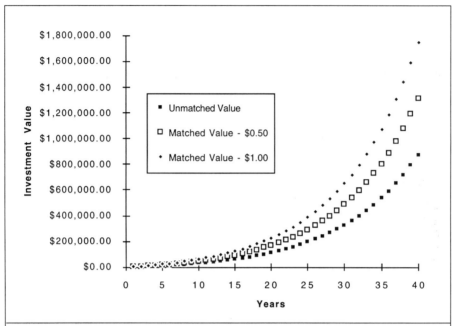

Notice how much greater your investment is worth when your employer matches your contribution. In this example, $1,800 is contributed each year for 40 years at a rate of 10 percent.

Ben starts off by investing his money for the first 10 years. After this period, he stops and lets the initial contribution grow for the remaining 30 years. Jerry, on the other hand, procrastinates. He waits 10 years before beginning to invest, but continues for the remaining 30. Both contribute $5,000 a year and earn 10 percent. Ben started earlier, but Jerry contributed for a longer time. Who do you suppose will have the greater account value? Ben who started early, or Jerry who put in three times as much?

Jerry, the procrastinator, will end up with $822,470. Ben will end up with $1,390,492. That's a difference of $568,022! Ben will be able to buy an awful lot more ice cream than Jerry! Now, what's the moral of the story? It is more important that you participate in your 401(k) the first one-third of your working life than the last two-thirds. This is a very important.

How To Build Wealth With Your 401(k)

It is more important that you participate in your 401(k) the first one-third of your working life than the last two-thirds!

NOTE: You may not have had a 401(k) early in your career because it is a relatively new retirement benefit. Don't let this disappoint you. Instead, tell your children to take advantage of the 401(k) their employer provides. This bit of advice could prove to be more valuable than if you were to leave them a sizeable inheritance.

The 401(k) is also a good accumulation vehicle when you are close to retirement because it offers the benefit of tax deferral. This is especially useful towards the end of your career because you are probably in a higher tax bracket. When you do retire and begin taking distributions from your 401(k) account, you may have the added tax advantage of being in a lower tax bracket. It's important to note that you should expect to invest for another 20 years after you retire.

Rule 2: Contribute Often

Now suppose Ben forgets to stop contributing at 10 years and accidentally contributes for the entire 40 years. Assume he still puts $5,000 away each year and earns 10 percent. What do you suppose his investment will be worth at age 65? $2,212,962! WOW! You wouldn't want to do that by accident! If your salary increases over time with raises, you will have even more money to invest and your final account value will actually be greater.

Rule 3: Invest Wisely

Starting early and contributing often is a very important step in wealth building but you must also choose your investments wisely. Even if you and a coworker invest the same amount of money in your company's retirement plan you could end up hundreds of thousands of dollars apart because of the investments you choose. In the remaining chapters I will walk you step-by-step through the investment process.

How to Get Money Out of Your Account

Hardship And In-Service Withdrawals

401(k) plans are allowed to offer withdrawals to employees who are still working and do not qualify for retirement withdrawals. A withdrawal of pre-tax contributions from an employee's account is called a hardship withdrawal. It is subject to ordinary income taxes plus a 10 percent penalty. If you become disabled you can withdraw money without the penalty but you are still subject to ordinary income taxes. A second type of withdrawal associated with after-tax contributions is called an in-service withdrawal. Your plan document explains the rules and different ways to take a withdrawal.

To qualify for hardship withdrawals you typically must show an immediate and significant financial need. The size of the distribution must match the need. The following expenses are considered to qualify:

(1) Medical expenses previously incurred by the employee, the employee's spouse or the employee's dependents, or expenses mandated for these individuals to obtain medical care.

(2) Expenses related to the purchase of the employee's principle residence (not including mortgage payments).

(3) Tuition and related educational fees for the next 12 months of post-secondary education for the employee or the employee's spouse or dependents.

(4) Payments to prevent eviction of the employee from a principle residence or payments to prevent foreclosure of the employee's principle residence.

The hardship withdrawal is subject to a 10 percent penalty as well as ordinary income taxes. If you receive a withdrawal you will probably not be eligible to make contributions into any of your employer's retirement plans for a 12 month period. (the IRS does not want you to pull money out then continue to contribute on a tax-deferred basis). Since you are not eligible to make contributions for one year you will also lose the opportunity to get any company matching funds if available. This is a fairly drastic set of conditions you are subject to when withdrawing funds. It is more favorable to take a loan if the plan allows it.

The in-service withdrawal is usually easy to get. Part of your withdrawal comes from money you contributed on an after-tax basis. This portion is not taxable again. A second part of your withdrawal comes from investment gain. This portion is subject to ordinary income taxes plus the 10 percent penalty. A pro-rata formula is used to determine the percentage you receive from after-tax contributions and investment gain.

Loans

You can also loan yourself money from your 401(k). There is no tax penalty and the interest rate must be reasonable. All the interest and principle of your loan payments go back into your account in after-tax dollars. The loan can be paid back in incremental payments within a specified time period, or you can use a lump sum to repay the balance at any time. The IRS restricts loans to 50 percent of an account value, or $50,000, whichever is less. Not all plans allow loans. Check your SPD.

Rollovers

You may roll over your company's qualified plan to another qualified plan and maintain the tax preference. There are two ways to do this.

(1) Direct rollover. The new plan receives the money directly from the original agent.

(2) Rollover paid to you. A rollover paid to you occurs when your plan is liquidated and the money is sent to you. You then have 60 days to put the money in a tax qualified plan or trigger taxes and penalties.

The rules for rollovers have changed. In the past you could receive your account value and do anything you wanted with the money for up to 60 days. You then had to put the money in a tax qualified plan or suffer the tax consequences.

The new rollover rules are much stricter. If you receive a rollover paid to you the plan must deduct 20 percent of the account value for income tax liability. Only then will you receive the balance. Once you receive the balance, you must put it in a qualified plan within 60 days or trigger further taxes and penalties.

You may get the 20 percent that was taxed back by coming up with the money out of your own account and depositing it into the qualified plan with the other 80 percent. You can then receive the 20 percent when you file your income taxes.

Don't do this! Use a direct agent rollover, not a rollover paid to you.

The definition for a rollover can be confusing. The proper definitions are given above. The key to remember is to use a direct rollover from qualified plan to qualified plan to avoid taxes. If you are eligible for a lump sum distribution, then be sure to read Chapter 8 which explains lump sum distributions options in detail.

Government Regulations

There are two federal agencies governing 401(k) plans. The Department of Labor is responsible for the protection of employees and sets regulations to ensure all employees receive fair treatment. It also ensures that companies comply with the Employee Retirement Income Securities Act (ERISA) which was passed to protect employees. The Internal Revenue Service is responsible for assuring compliance with the internal revenue code.

Government regulations are designed to guide the start-up and operation of a 401(k) plan. A company is not required to establish a 401(k) plan, but if it does it must follow the guidelines. Once a 401(k) plan is established, it is not required to have all the available features and it may establish more conservative rules than those outlined by the government.

For example, the plan does not have to allow loans. If it does, it may lower the limit to less than 50 percent of the account balance where 50 percent is the cap established by the government. As a second example, the company can place a limit on the amount you can contribute to the plan and this limit can be lower than what the government allows. Of course the company can't allow you to contribute more than what is allowed by the government. And, as a final example, the company is not required to make matching contributions on behalf of employees.

ERISA Rules And Regulations

ERISA rules and regulations apply to both pension and contribution plans. We will limit our discussion to contribution plans as we discuss the following topics: disclosure and reporting; eligibility; vesting; funding; fiduciary responsibility; and beneficiaries.

Disclosure And Reporting

Employee benefit plan sponsors are required to supply a Summary Plan Description (SPD). This document must contain enough information to inform participants about plan operations and beneficiaries' rights. You are also entitled to a yearly benefit statement which will give you a statement of your account. The IRS requires that the company administrator files form 5500 which contains plan investment information.

Eligibility to Participate

You are generally eligible to participate in your employer's 401(k) if you are over eighteen and have completed one year of service. One year of service is defined as 1,000 hours of work in any twelve month period. Plans cannot require the employee to be over 21 or have more than one year of service. The one exception is for plans that offer immediate vesting. In this case, it is okay to require two years of service to become eligible.

Vesting

You are immediately vested in the funds you contribute to the plan. This means that whatever you put in belongs to you. The company matching funds may be subject to vesting rules. These rules have been established by the company under ERISA guidelines.

A company can choose to allow immediate vesting, but more commonly chooses either a five- or seven-year vesting schedule. With the five-year schedule, you are 100 percent vested after five years of service. With the seven year schedule, you are 20 percent vested at three years and vested an additional 20 percent incrementally until full vesting is reached after seven years.

If you leave the company voluntarily or are fired prior to vesting, all company matched funds are typically forfeited. If you are laid off, it is the company's option whether or not to give you the company matched portion of your savings. Of course, the vested portion is yours to keep. In most cases you will receive the non-vested money after a layoff.

Funding

Qualified contribution plans must be established by a trust in the employees name. All funds are maintained by the trust. Employee contributions must be made into the employee's account within 15 days of the month following the month the checks were paid.

Fiduciary Responsibility

The 401(k) is set up as a trust in your name. The company must choose investment options in the best interest of the employee. The options selected must be reasonable. No matter what happens to the company, your 401(k) is safe because it is a separate entity. In other words, if the company fails, your account is not lost.

Beneficiaries

You have the right to assign your account to a beneficiary. If you are married and choose not to assign your spouse, then the spouse must sign a waiver of rights.

Tax Restrictions

The Internal Revenue Code (IRC) places certain restrictions on contribution plans. The rules are established to assure all employees receive equal benefits. Certain rules are designed to prevent highly compensated employees from receiving greater benefits. Two tax restrictions regarding contributions to defined contribution plans that affect you are:

(1) The maximum amount of money that can be made to a qualified plan is 25 percent of an employee's salary or $30,000 per year.

(2) The maximum amount an employee can defer a year is $9,500 in 1997. This amount is indexed to inflation.

Find Out What Your Own Plan Is All About

Your company is required to provide you with a Summary Plan Description (SPD) document. The SPD contains information about how your plan is set up along with information about investment options and performance.

Your company should also provide you with a statement of benefits each year. Most employers send them out in late January. The statement period covers the previous calendar year ending December 31. The Statement of Benefits contains important information about your contributions, matching funds, account allocation, and vested money. You should keep all your statements.

You may also get a copy of the IRS form 5500 that the plan administrator must file. It contains more detailed information required by the IRS. Your benefits department may charge you copying expenses for the form if you want to keep it. The form must be available for you to review without charge.

401(k) plans vary from company to company. Some may offer better features than others. As the 401(k) has become more popular, the features have improved. The areas that make your 401(k) different from another company's plan are: eligibility, vesting schedules, contribution rates, investment options, withdrawals, loans, and transfers. Use the worksheets presented in the next few pages to gather information on the unique characteristics of your 401(k) plan.

Some of the information you need to complete the worksheets can be found in your Summary Plan Description or in your benefits statement. You will likely need the assistance of your benefits administrator to obtain other types of information.

Your company's benefits personnel are not always able to answer all your questions. For instance, they will not (and should not!) give you investment advice such as telling you where to put your money. They should, however, give you all the information you need to make informed investment decisions. Do not settle for the answer "I don't know" or "We don't have that information". Their job is to get it for you. I have seen both extremes of cooperation from benefits personnel. Some go out of their way to help you obtain the information you need. Others go out of their way to make things difficult. In either event, the information is available, it just may require a little more digging.

Don't be overwhelmed by the amount of information you need to collect. As you read through this book, you will be very glad to have it all at your fingertips. The fun part comes in the last few chapters when you finally have enough background information to analyze your own accounts and make allocation decisions. Collecting the information adds to your education. Just remember, he who has the most knowledge usually fairs best. Information is the leverage you need to accumulate great wealth.

Do You Have a 403(b), 457, or Federal Thrift Savings Plan?

The rules and regulations for a 403(b), 457 and Thrift Savings Plan are slightly different than those governing a 401(k) plan. The worksheets in Table 2.2 will provide you with the information you need, but there may be some differences. Keep in mind that selecting and analyzing an investment are the same regardless of which plan you have. If you are in a 403(b) plan, refer to Appendix C for more information.

Table 2.2   Company Unique 401(k) Worksheet

Eligibility	
Am I eligible to participate in my company's 401(k)? Most employers make you wait at least one year.	
Vesting Schedule	
What type of vesting schedule is in place, five or seven year?	
Contribution Rates	
What is the maximum percent of salary that can be pre-tax-deferred into the plan?	
Up to what percent does my employer match my contribution?	
What is the minimum percentage that can be allocated to a fund?	
How are past contributions handled if I change my investment selection? Will past contributions remain in the same investment or be moved to the new contribution investment selection?	
Are there any funds that I can't move my money out of? Some fixed income funds do not allow you to move your money within a certain time period.	
Are there any restrictions on moving money between different funds? Some funds have restrictions on where they can be moved to.	
How often can I move money between funds?	
What is the time delay before the money is actually moved?	

Table 2.2 Cont.   Company Unique 401(k) Worksheet

Investment Options	
How many investment options do I have?	
What type of options are available (bond funds, equity funds, diversified stock fund, index fund, fixed income, GIC, money market)?	
Who manages the funds and where are the assets allocated (mutual funds, insurers in a GIC, investment advisors)? You should be able to get a prospectus on each fund along with any other literature that describes each fund and it's objective.	
What is the past performance of each fund and how often can I find out about fund performance? Get the annual rate of return for each fund year ending Dec 31. Get as many years as possible.	
How often can I change options (quarterly, monthly)?	
What are the conditions (30 days notice prior to quarter, end of month)?	
How do I change investment options, by telephone or written change request ?	
What expenses am I paying for the administration of the plan?	
What are the expenses of each fund (administration, management, other)? Do I pay a front- or back-end sales load? All funds charge a management fee that varies between 0.5 percent and 2 percent.	

Table 2.2 Cont.   Company Unique 401(k) Worksheet

Loans, Withdrawals & Distributions	
Are loans available?	
If a loan is taken, can I still contribute to the plan, or am I suspended for some period of time?	
How long will it take to get my loan processed?	
If I make a withdrawal, am I suspended from making contributions to the plan?	
When I retire, will my employer allow me to keep my money in the 401(k)? If so, can I move money between funds and can I make withdrawals?	
If I leave my job and maintain my account what are the restrictions on account transactions? Can I request a direct rollover at a later time? If your account value is greater than $3,500, your employer cannot make you take a distribution, but there may be restrictions on your account. You will learn more about this subject in Chapter 8.	
When I retire, will the plan providers calculate the minimum withdrawals required?	
When I retire, can I make a direct transfer from my account into an IRA? See Chapter 8 for more information.	

Table 2.2 Cont.   Company Unique 401(k) Worksheet

Personal Calculations	
Step 1 What percent of my salary can I tax defer? **Example**: Company A allows 12% of base salary to be contributed pre-tax into the company 401(k) plan.	
Step 2 What dollar amount can I defer? **Example:** An employee earning $50,000 a year at Company A can defer 0.12 x $50,000 = $6,000.	**dollar amount of your deferred savings** = Step 1 x (your annual salary)
Step 3 What is my tax savings if I defer the maximum amount? **Example:** 28% tax bracket, $6,000 x 0.28 = $1,680	**your tax savings** = Step 2 x (your tax bracket as a %)
Step 4 What dollar amount does my employer match my contributions?	
Step 5 What percent of my salary will they match? **Example:** Match $1 on the first 6% of contributions.	NOTE: some plans do not match on a % of your base salary. Instead, a formula may be used that matches at different rates across your base salary. A match may be 8% of the first $10,000 of salary and 6% for the amount above $10,000. If this is the case, skip this question and use your company's formula to calculate the dollar amount requested in the next question.

Table 2.2 Cont.   Company Unique 401(k) Worksheet

Personal Calculations	
Step 6 What is the dollar amount of my salary that my employer will match? **Example**: 6% match, 0.06 x $50,000 = $3,000	**dollar amount of your salary that is matched** = Step 5 x (your annual salary)
Step 7 What is the total dollar amount that my company will contribute? **Example**: $1 x $3,000 = $3,000	**dollar amount that your company contributes** = Step 4 x Step 6
Step 8 What is the total dollar amount available for me to invest in my 401(k)? **Example**: $6,000 + $3,000 = $9,000	**total dollar amount available to invest in your 401(k)** = Step 2 + Step 7

Chapter 3

The Starting Point for All Investors

Definition and Stages of Investing

An investment is a place you put your money, assume some risk, and expect a positive increase in value. You invest because you expect to earn a profit on your money. By investing some money today, you will have more money to spend tomorrow. Investing is the foundation of a free market society. Investors have excess funds available to loan to borrowers. Lenders and borrowers can be businesses, governments, or individuals.

Businesses may need to borrow capital to expand plant capacity or open new markets. Governments borrow money to support programs such as building roads and bridges. Individuals borrow money to buy houses, cars, and other consumer items. In turn, consumer borrowing spurs the need to build things such as roads and bridges. More jobs are added and the economy grows.

Investors provide the funds that satisfy borrowers. There are investments available to match every type of borrowing need. So how do you know which is best for you? You must begin by examining your own needs. What is your overall objective for investing? Are you saving for retirement? Do you want to build up funds to put your children through college? Or are you at a point where you need current income? What's your risk tolerance? Do you have special tax considerations? And what are the consequences if you need to liquidate your investment?

The first stage of investing, **accumulation,** is when you start earning more than you need to live on. It is difficult to determine this exact moment in time. You can always seem to find a "need" to spend excess cash. It takes great discipline to begin an investing program. The separation of "needs" and "desires" is an eternal struggle of mankind.

Your ability to start accumulating cash early will be directly proportional to the quality of life you live later.

The second stage of investing, **growth**, starts at the same time you begin accumulating investment funds. This stage requires a long time horizon so that compound interest can work its magic. You should expect the growth stage to continue even as you make periodic withdrawals and until your investment is completely depleted.

The last stage is **withdrawal**. It begins when you want to dip into your accumulated funds for something such as retirement, college, a new house, a vacation or just to supplement income. Don't forget, you still want your investment to grow even as you make partial withdrawals. Typically you're still in a growth stage even though you're withdrawing funds.

You must continue to at least keep pace with inflation during your withdrawal period. If not, the value of your investment will diminish at the rate of inflation.

All investment decisions are yours to make. It's up to you to ensure your money is wisely and appropriately invested. There is no one on the face of the earth that cares more about your financial security then you.

You are 100 percent responsible for your investment outcome whether you invest the money yourself or you give it to someone to invest for you.

With responsibility comes opportunity. You have the ability to fulfill your financial goals. Knowledge is the key to your success. The remainder of this book is devoted to giving you the information you need to become a wise investor. The only way to guarantee success is to continually educate yourself in the practice of investing.

Investment Objectives

Several ideas must be understood before you are ready to make informed investment decisions. Let's start by looking at investment objectives. People invest for one or more of five general reasons: (1) to accumulate money for big expenses, such as a down payment on a house, a new car, or to finance a child's education, (2) to increase income, (3) to gain wealth and a feeling of financial security, (4) to have money available during retirement years, and (5) to maximize income during retirement.

The first step is to decide what you expect to gain from investing. You need to determine exactly how much money you want to accumulate and the time in which you need it. From here you can estimate the amount of money you need to invest and the rate of return you need. This information is used to determine which investment selections are best for you. Table 3.1 gives examples of common objectives and time frames.

Table 3.1   Typical Investment Objectives

Typical Objectives	Time Frame
Save for a new house	5 years
Finance a child's college education	10-15- years
Accumulate funds for retirement	25-30 years
Maximize savings during retirement	20-25 years
Think about what you need the money for before you start your investment program.	

Time Value of Money

The time horizon for investing should be at least five years. You must provide sufficient time for the investment to grow and for market fluctuations to occur. The more time given for an investment to grow, the greater its growth potential and the lower it's risk.

Time is an investor's best friend.

Time value of money is an extremely important subject. It refers to the impact that compound interest has on your investment. **Compound interest** is interest paid not only on the initial deposit but also on any interest accumulated from one period to the next. The sooner you receive a return on your money the better because it has more time to compound.

Compound interest allows you to take a small amount of money and over time turn it into a large fortune.

Liquidity

Liquidity is the ability to cash out of an investment. Some investments are difficult to liquefy. Real estate may take months or years to unload so it's not considered very liquid. And there are some investments you can't unload at any price. For example, limited partnerships that were popular in the 1980's are almost impossible to give away.

Liquidity measures the ease of getting out of an investment. If you need to sell when the financial market is in a down cycle, you'll end up losing money. That's why it's best to have at least a five year time horizon so that you can ride out downturns in the market.

If you need the money in a short time, say one to two years, then you shouldn't be investing in long-term investments such as stocks, bonds, and real estate. You should put the money in a cash equivalent investment.

The investor who was in the stock market at the beginning of 1987 and sold immediately after the October 1987 drop lost money. Those that stayed invested in the market ended the year with an average 5 percent gain!

Investment Return

We invest to make more money. The "extra" money beyond what we put in is called a **return**. There are two types of investment returns, current income and capital appreciation. Current income is a cash distribution paid periodically in the form of interest or dividend payouts. The payouts may be at a set rate and time or they may vary with the investment's performance.

Capital appreciation is an increase in the value of your investment. If you purchase an investment for $1,000 and one year later it's worth $1,200, you have a capital appreciation of $200. You realize a **capital gain** when the investment is sold. If the value of your investment is lower when you sell it then when you purchased it, then you have a **capital loss.**

An investment's **total return** is the sum total of current income and capital appreciation. You can measure the return on your investment by comparing its starting value to its ending value over the time you held the investment. Let's look at an example. Let's say you made an investment of $1,000. After the investment period was over, your investment was worth $1,100. This includes interest, capital gains and principle. What is the return on your investment?

Return = (ending value / beginning value) - 1
        = ($1,100 / $1,000) - 1
        = 0.10, or 10%

This example looks at an investment over a holding period without regard to time. If the holding period was one year, a 10 percent return would be very good. If the holding period was five years, the 10 percent return would not have been very good.

Which holding period would you prefer for a $1,000 investment, 1 year or 5 years?

Compound Interest

Let's look at an example of compound interest. An initial $1,000 investment earning 10 percent per year will earn $100 interest after the first year giving a total of $1,100. At the end of the second year the initial $1,000 investment will earn another $100, and the original $100 interest will earn an additional $10. This gives the investor a total of $110 interest earned the second year, and an investment total of $1,210. You can see from Figure 3.1 and Figure 3.2 how compound interest helps your investment grow dramatically over time.

Figure 3.1   The Power of Compound Interest

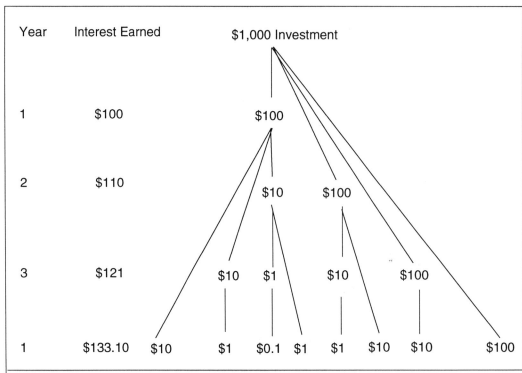

Each dollar of interest you earn goes toward making more interest. Over time, this can translates into a large sum of money.

Figure 3.2 $1 Growing 10 Percent Per Year

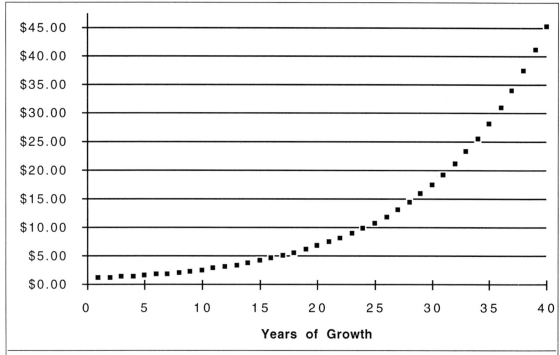

Years of Growth

The longer you hold your investment, the greater impact compound interest has on the growth of your savings. In this figure you can see that $1 is worth $45 after 40 years of growing at 10 percent.

The Two Most Important Calculations You'll Ever Need to Know

How would you like to know what your current savings will be worth at some time in the future if you let it continue to grow on its own or if you continually add money to it each year? In other words, you know how much money you have today so you would like to know what it will be worth in the future. Now that you understand compound interest you know the answers are not straight forward.

Expert money managers perform these kind of calculations on a routine basis. Now its time for real-life investors (like yourself!) to learn how as well. To answer these questions you need to calculate the **future value** of your investment. To begin, get yourself a simple calculator that performs multiplication and get ready to use the Future Value Tables in Appendix A-1 and A-2 at the end of this book.

Wouldn't it also be nice to know the amount of savings you must have today in order to generate the account value you want when you retire? And if you don't currently have this much money, wouldn't it be nice to know the amount of annual contributions you must make instead? To solve this problem you need to calculate the **present value** of your savings. When calculating present value you know how much money you want at some time in the future and you are estimating how much money you need now to get there. All you need is a simple calculator and the Present Value Tables in Appendix A-3 and A-4

Future value and present value can also be calculated using a financial calculator or a spreadsheet with the functions built in. If you already have access to theses tools, great, If not, there's no need to run out and buy them because the lookup tables at the end of this book are just about as easy to use.

Future Value of a Single Payment

Let's say you make a single payment into an investment and want to find out what it will be worth in the future taking into account compound interest. You will need to calculate the future value of your investment, or the **future value of a single payment**. This is sometimes referred to as the future value of a lump sum.

$$FV = PV \times FVIF$$

n = number of years your investment is allowed to grow

r = rate of return you expect to receive

PV = The initial dollar amount of the single payment

$FVIF$ = Future Value Interest Factor found by looking up n and r in Appendix A-1

The first thing you do is look up FVIF in Appendix A-1. FVIF is a multiplier used to determine the growth of $1 over a given number of periods at a given rate of return. Appendix A-1 has the FVIF already calculated. Look up FVIF by using the given period and rate of return. The rate of return is listed as a percentage and the corresponding period is in years.

Once you have found FVIF, plug it into the formula along with the dollar amount of your single payment and you get the future value of your investment for n periods at r rate of return.

Let's find a few FVIF's for different periods and interest rates.

Example 1   What is the FVIF for n = 10 and r = 10?

From Appendix A-1, find where n = 10 and r = 10 intersect.

The FVIF = 2.594

Example 2   What is FVIF for n = 8, r= 12?

From Appendix A-1, find where n = 8 and r = 12 intersect.

The FVIF = 2.476.

Example 3   Find FVIF for n = 5, r = 10

FVIF = 1.611

Example 4   Find FVIF for n = 7, r = 3

FVIF = 1.230

Now let's calculate FV in a few examples.

Example 5   If a single payment of $10,000 is made to an investment, what is the value of the investment after 10 years if it earns an annual interest rate of 10 percent?

From Appendix A-1 we find FVIF = 2.594 when n = 10 and r = 10

FV = PV x FVIF = $10,000 x 2.594 = $25,940

This example shows that if you make a single investment of $10,000 and let it grow for 10 years at a rate of 10 percent, your investment will be worth $25,940 at the end of the 10 years.

What is the future value of a single payment investment of $100,000 earning 6 percent annual rate of return after 10, 20, 30, & 40 years? See Table 3.2 for the answers. What is the value of the investment if it earned 10 percent over the same periods? See Table 3.3 for the answers.

Table 3.2   **Future Value Exercise**

	example 1	example 2	example 3	example 4
r	6	6	6	6
n	10	20	30	40
FVIF	1.791	3.207	5.743	10.286
FV	$179,100	$320,700	$574,300	$1,028,600

Practice calculating the Future Value (FV) of a single payment with these exercises. The single payment is $100,000. Where r = the interest rate, n equals the number of years and FVIF equals the Future Value Investment Factor found in Appendix A-1.

Table 3.3   **More Future Value Exercises**

	example 1	example 2	example 3	example 4
r	10	10	10	10
n	10	20	30	40
FVIF	2.594	6.727	17.449	45.259
FV	$259,400	$672,700	$1,744,900	$4,525,900

Practice calculating the Future Value (FV) of a single payment with these exercises. The single payment is $100,000. Where r = the interest rate, n equals the number of years and FVIF equals the Future Value Investment Factor found in Appendix A-1.

The difference in the rate of return you receive on your investment has an incredible impact on the final value of your account. As the investment time period gets longer, the difference between a few percentage points makes an amazing difference. Let's look at an example.

Tables 3.2 and 3.3 both show the future value of a $100,000 single payment over a 10, 20, 30, and 40 year investment period. Table 3.2 shows a 6 percent annual rate of return. Table 3.3 shows a 10 percent annual rate of return.

Look at the future value in both tables after 10 years. The 10 percent return has a much higher future value than the 6 percent return, which seems obvious, but let's look further. After 20 years, the 10 percent return is *double* the 6 percent return.

After 40 years, the 10 percent return is *4.5 times greater* than the 6 percent return! Even though both investments started out with the same initial payment of $100,000, the account earning 4 percentage points higher has *$3.5 million more dollars in it!* Now you can really see what the power of compound interest is all about.

Table 3.3 shows that a $100,000 dollar investment earning 10 percent will give you $1,744,900 after 30 years. This would certainly be a nice retirement nest egg. The only problem is that most people don't have $100,000 to plunk down 30 years before retirement. The single payment investment is not exactly a realistic approach to starting your retirement savings. It's best to use this calculation to estimate what your current savings will be worth when you retire.

Future Value of an Annuity

With future value of a single payment you are able to calculate how much a lump sum investment will be worth in the future based on a given interest rate. Let's look at what happens when you make smaller, periodic payments over time instead of plunking down one lump sum.

A series of equal payments at fixed intervals is called an **annuity**. An example of an annuity is a payment of $1,000 per year for 10 years. After 10 years you would have contributed $10,000 to the investment. The total value of the investment is the sum of the payments plus return on the investment.

You can calculate the future value of an annuity investment with the same types of tools used to calculate the future value of a single payment. One way would be to use the single payment tables and find the value of the investment after each of the 10 years as used in the above example and add them up. This could be very tedious. Fortunately there is an easier way.

FVA = PMT x FVAIF

n = number of years the investment is allowed to grow

r = the rate of return you expect to receive

PMT = Continual payment made each year in dollars

FVAIF = Future Value Annuity Investment Factor, from Appendix A-2

Example 1   Suppose you plan to contribute $1,000 per year to a mutual fund that is expected to return 10 percent annually over the next 10 years. What is the future value of your investment after 10 years?

From Appendix A-2 we find FVAIF = 15.937 when n = 10 and r = 10.

FVA = PMT x FVAIF = $1,000 x 15.937 = $15,937

You contributed $10,000 in equal payments over 10 years. The additional $5,937 is the compound interest earned over the 10 years.

Present Value of a Single Payment

We have talked about the future value of money. The examples showed how the principle of compound interest increases the value of your investment over time. You have also seen how to calculate the future value of both a single payment and an annuity payment. Now let's look at it from the other angle. If you know how much money you want to have at the end of a given number of years, how much money do you need now in order to reach this goal? To answer this question you need to calculate the present value of a single payment using Appendix A-3.

PV = FV x PVIF

n = number of years the investment is allowed to grow

r = the rate of return you expect to receive

FV = the desired future value of your investment

PVIF is the Present Value Factor found in Appendix A-3

Example 1   Let's say you wish to have an investment value of $100,000 in 20 years. What is the present value of a single payment investment if the annual return is 10 percent?

From Appendix A-3 we find PVIF = 0.149 for n = 20 and r = 10.

PV = FV x PVIF = $100,000 x 0.149 = $14,900

Present Value of an Annuity

When calculating the present value of a single payment you start by knowing how much money you want at some time in the future. If you would rather receive a stream of income that extends into the future instead of a lump sum that you receive at a give year in the future, you can calculate the present value of an annuity. In this case you know the amount of annual income you want to start receiving today and you are calculating the lump sum needed in order to generate this cash flow.

PVA = PMT x PVAIF

n = number of years the investment is allowed to grow

r = the rate of return you expect to receive

PMT = annuity payment

PVAIF = Present Value Annuity Interest Factor found in Appendix A-4 using the given number of years, n and the given rate of return, r.

Example 1   What is the present value of an annuity investment that will pay $1,000 per year for 20 years? Assume an annual rate of return of 10 percent.

From Appendix A-4 we find PVAIF = 8.514 for n = 20 and r = 10

PVA = PMT x PVAIF = $1,000 x 8.514 = $8,514

Would you rather have a lump sum of $10,000 or a annuity payment of $1,000 per year for 20 years? From our example we see that the present value of the annuity payment is only worth $8,514. A lump sum of $10,000 can be invested at the same rate of return and be worth more after 20 years. Use Appendix A-1 and determine what a $10,000 single payment will be worth in 20 years.

Why is the $10,000 lump sum investment worth more after 20 years than the $20,000 worth of annuity payments over 20 years at the same rate of return? *Because of the power of compound interest!* The $10,000 investment had a longer time to compound. The annuity payments only compounded for the time in which they were invested. This calculation is useful when evaluating annuitization over lump sum distribution.

Now that you are familiar with the power of compound interest let's look at an illustration. Table 3.4 shows how important it is to start investing early and to continue making contributions over a long period of time. If you start early and invest often, you can turn a small amount of money into a large fortune.

How to Estimate the Future Value of Your 401(k)

There are a few calculations important to the management of your 401(k) account. First, you need to know how much money you can get into your account. This includes your employer's contributions as well as your own. Second, you need to be able to estimate what the value of your account will be in the future. And third, you will find it very useful to calculate how much you need to contribute to your 401(k) in order to reach future goals. Let's look at an example.

Jay is 35 years old, makes $30,000 a year, and plans to retire at age 65 . His employer allows pre-tax 401(k) contributions of up to 12 percent of gross salary. Jay also receives a 100 percent match for contributions up to 6 percent of his gross salary. How much can Jay get into his 401(k) and what will the future value of his account be in 30 years if his contributions remain the same each year?

Step 1 How much money can Jay get into his 401(k)? Be sure to include Jay's contributions as well as his employer's.

The maximum amount Jay can contribute is 12 percent of his gross salary or $30,000 x 0.12 = $3,600. This means that Jay can contribute up to $3,600 per year into his 401(k) account.

The company match is $1.00 for each dollar Jay contributes up to 6 percent of his gross salary, or $30,000 x 0.06 = $1,800. In other words, Jay's employer will contribute up to $1,800 into Jay's account. By adding Jay's annual contribution of $3,600 to his employer's annual contribution of $1,800, you get the total amount of money that Jay can get into his account. The final value is $3,600 + $1,800 = $5,400.

Matching employer contributions is a very valuable benefit. You should always contribute at least as much as needed to get the full match.

Table 3.4　Start Early and Invest Continually

Year	Early Investment	Delayed Investment	Continual Early Investment
1	$5,000.00		$5,000.00
2	$10,500.00		$10,500.00
3	$16,550.00		$16,550.00
4	$23,205.00		$23,205.00
5	$30,525.50		$30,525.50
6	$38,578.05		$38,578.05
7	$47,435.86		$47,435.86
8	$57,179.44		$57,179.44
9	$67,897.38		$67,897.38
10	$79,687.12		$79,687.12
11		$5,000.00	$92,655.84
12		$10,500.00	$106,921.42
13		$16,550.00	$122,613.56
14		$23,205.00	$139,874.92
15		$30,525.50	$158,862.41
16		$38,578.05	$179,748.65
17		$47,435.86	$202,723.51
18		$57,179.44	$227,995.87
19		$67,897.38	$255,795.45
20		$79,687.12	$286,375.00
21		$92,655.84	$320,012.50
22		$106,921.42	$357,013.75
23		$122,613.56	$397,715.12
24		$139,874.92	$442,486.63
25		$158,862.41	$491,735.30
26		$179,748.65	$545,908.83
27		$202,723.51	$605,499.71
28		$227,995.87	$671,049.68
29		$255,795.45	$743,154.65
30		$286,375.00	$822,470.11
31		$320,012.50	$909,717.12
32		$357,013.75	$1,005,688.84
33		$397,715.12	$1,111,257.72
34		$442,486.63	$1,227,383.49
35		$491,735.30	$1,355,121.84
36		$545,908.83	$1,495,634.03
37		$605,499.71	$1,650,197.43
38		$671,049.68	$1,820,217.17
39		$743,154.65	$2,007,238.89
40	$1,390,492.66	$822,470.11	$2,212,962.78
Total Principle	$50,000.00	$150,000.00	$200,000.00
Total Interest	$1,340,492.66	$672,470.11	$2,012,962.78

If you start investing early, you will end up with more money than if you start late and contribute more. This illustration assumes 10 percent annual return on a $5,000 annual investment

Remember that Jay's contribution is tax deferred. If Jay is in the 28 percent tax bracket, then his tax savings for the current year is $3,600 x 0.28 = $1,008. If Jay is in the 15 percent tax bracket then his tax savings is $3,600 x 0.15 = $540. Not a bad tax break for an opportunity to build wealth!

Step 2 Estimate the future value of Jay's 401(k) account.

Using the solution from step one we know Jay can get $5,400 per year into his 401(k) account. Assuming a 10 percent average annual rate of return, and 30 years until retirement what would Jay's account value be at retirement?

Since we are projecting the future value of a series of constant payments ($5,400) for a defined period (30 years), we are calculating the future value of an annuity.

FVA = PMT x FVAIF

FVAIF = 164.494 for n = 30 years, r = 10% (from Appendix A-2)

FVA = PMT x FVAIF = $5,400 x 164.494 = $888,267.60

In other words, the future value of Jay's account after 30 years of contributing $5,400 per year and earning an average 10 percent rate of return is $888,267.60. If the average annual rate of return is 6 percent instead of 10 percent, Jay's final account value would be worth only $426,914 which is less than half the value. The difference in interest rates over a long period of time has a tremendous affect on the final value of your account.

Suppose Jay has $10,000 already in his account prior to starting the 30 years of $5,400 payments. What would the future value of his account be if he were to include the initial $10,000? In step two we have already calculated the annuity value of his annual payments over thirty years. The next step is to calculate the future value of the $10,000 as a single payment and add it to the future value of the annuity to get the total account value.

FV = PV x FVIF

FVIF = 17.449 for n= 30 years, and r = 10% (from Appendix A-1)

FV = PV x FVIF = $10,000 x 17.449 = $174,490

In 30 years, when Jay is 65, his $10,000 single payment will grow to $174,490. Add this to the $888,267.60 that came from his $5,400 per year contribution and Jay has a total final account value of $1,062,757.60. Of course the actual future value of his account could be higher or lower depending on the actual performance of his investments and the contributions made.

Keep in mind that your contributions will likely increase as your salary increases. It is a good idea to periodically (every few years) reestimate your future account value as your fund grows and your contribution level changes.

Your account will build up slowly when you first start out. It takes time for compounding interest to start it's rapid growth. Look back at Table 3.4 to see the growth you can expect if you start early.

Lets look at the final account value from another angle. Suppose Jay currently has no money in his account, but wants his 401(k) to be worth $1,000,000 when he reaches age 65. What payment level would be required to reach this amount if we assume a 10 percent average annual rate of return? Use the formula $FVA(n, r) = Payment \times FVAIF$.

$PMT = FVA / FVAIF$

$FVAIF = 164.494$ (for n = 30 years and r = 10%)

$PMT = FVA / FVAIF = \$1,000,000 / 164.494 = \$6,079.25$

Assuming Jay started with no money in his account, annual contributions of $6,079.25 for 30 years at 10 percent will allow him to accumulate $1,000,000. See Table 3.5 for a summary of future value and present value calculations.

Table 3.5   Summary of Present Value and Future Value Calculations

Value you are solving for	Information you already have	Value from Appendix	Use this formula when...
future value of a single payment $FV = PV \times FVIF$	PV - the dollar amount you currently have as a single payment or lump sum	FVIF, found by looking up n and r in Appendix A-1	You want to know what the lump sum of money you have today will be worth in the future
future value of an annuity $FVA = PMT \times FVAIF$	PMT - continual payment you plan to make into your investment each year	FVAIF found by looking up n and r in Appendix A-2	You want to know how much money you will have in the future if you make continuous equal payments until that time
present value of a single payment $PV = FV \times PVIF$	FV - the amount of money you wish to have at some time in the future	PVIF found by looking up n and r in Appendix A-3	You know how much money you wish to have at some time in the future and you want to know what lump sum you need today to reach your goal
present value of an annuity $PVA = PMT \times PVAIF$	PMT - annual income stream you want. You start receiving it today and it extends into the future.	PVAIF found by looking up n and r in Appendix A-4	You want to know what lump sum you need today in order to generate a continuous stream of income that starts today and extends into the future

This table summarizes everything you have learned about future value and present value calculations. Use it to refresh your memory any time you perform these calculations. In each scenario, the variables n and r are known. n is the number of years your investment is allowed to grow. r is the interest rate you think your investment will grow at. It is an assumed rate. There is no way to know in advance exactly what the annual interest rate will be. It's a good idea to practice "what if" scenarios where you perform the same calculation several times using different interest rates.

Inflation

Inflation is the increase in the price of consumer goods and services caused by a surplus of money in the hands of willing and able purchasers. Purchasers buy as many products as they can. The high demand causes a shortage of products since the factories can not keep up with the demand. This in turn drives the price of products upward. High demand and low supply leads to high prices.

Inflation erodes away your purchasing power over time. If the price of goods and services increase at a rate greater then your income, then you lose purchasing power. What you buy with a dollar today may cost as much as $1.20 in a couple of years. Your income must increase with inflation just to stay even with your ability to purchase goods and services. Inflation causes the real value of a dollar to decrease. Figure 3.3 shows the erosion of a dollar's value due to inflation since 1971. *A dollar earned in 1971 was worth only about 26 cents in 1992!*

We live in an inflationary time. Since the early 1960's inflation has been a major influence on our society.

Figure 3.3   Purchasing Power Of $1 Since 1971

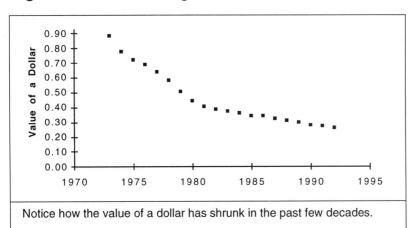

Notice how the value of a dollar has shrunk in the past few decades.

Inflation is a silent and dangerous partner to investing. If you are earning 3 percent on an investment and inflation is running 5 percent, you actually lose 2 percent. Likewise, if you earn 5 percent on an investment with an inflation rate of 5 percent, you end up breaking even. This is often a difficult idea to grasp. An investment may be safe and return your principle with some interest, but with inflation you can actually lose purchasing power.

How to Estimate Inflation

You can estimate inflation with a price index. Several price indexes exist. The most popular is the Consumer Price Index (CPI). The CPI is a government established "basket" of goods and services designed to represent the average consumer's purchases. This basket of goods and services is tracked and the difference in price is used to calculate inflation for that period in time.

The CPI is updated periodically to keep track with consumer trends. The base, or reference year, is also reestablished as required to keep the relative difference between base year and future years manageable. The basket of goods and services representing the CPI include things such as milk, eggs, haircuts, automobile, medical visits, clothing, and other types of consumer items.

The CPI assigns an index of 1.00 to the base year basket of goods. The same basket is sampled after some time and an index for that time is established. The new index is compared to the index of the base year. The outcome of the comparison is either an increase or decrease in price. An increase means we must pay more money for the same basket of goods. The CPI is typically expressed as an annual percentage rate.

The CPI has a few known shortfalls. Because the index represents an *average* basket of goods and services, it does not accurately measure inflation for everyone. Not everyone buys the same items found in the representative basket. Some may be frugal and better able to spend their dollar. Others may spend freely and end up with very little to show for their dollar.

The CPI is still considered the best available representation of inflation. Some studies suggest it overestimates inflation by about a half of a percentage point. But this doesn't matter as long as you know inflation exists and take precautions so that your investments out perform it.

Inflation has a stronger affect on investments held for a long time. Shorter time periods, six months to a year, do not suffer as much at the hands of inflation.

Taxes

Taxes are much more tangible to investors than inflation. You get a good feel for their affect every time you look at the money taken out of your paycheck. You can also be reminded of their liabilities when an interest paying investment has done well and April 15 is around the corner.

As an investor, you are only able to keep the after-tax portion of your investment return. It is important to have a basic understanding of the tax structure. Our government has probably developed the most difficult method possible to calculate tax liabilities. There is no way to discuss every aspect of taxation in this book. Taxes are unique to each situation and the rules and limits are constantly changing. But we will look at some basic concepts applicable to all investors.

You are probably familiar with the IRS tax brackets. Many working professionals are in the 28 percent tax bracket. This does not mean you pay 28 percent of your gross income in taxes. You actually pay less than that. Instead, 28 percent is the marginal tax rate at which the last incremental dollar of your income is taxed. This is important to understand because investment returns are typically taxed at the investor's marginal rate.

To better understand the marginal tax rate system lets look at an example. This example is very general and is only intended to show the affect of the marginal tax rate.

Mr. & Mrs. Investor have a family earned income of $50,000 a year. They file as married filing jointly. Their personal exemptions of $6,900 (3 x $2,300, for 1992 tax filers) plus mortgage interest and property taxes of $5,000 allow them to deduct a total of $11,900 from their adjusted gross income. This leaves them with a taxable income of $38,100 ($50,000 - $11,900). You can now use the tax schedule to calculate their tax liability.

Many tax filers use the pre-calculated tables supplied by the IRS. The tax owed is already calculated using the formula and put into tables at $50 increments.

Using 1992 tax rate Schedule Y-1, married filing jointly, to calculate the taxes owed by Mr. & Mrs. Investor. For a taxable income between $35,800 and $86,500 the tax is $5,370 + 28 percent of the amount over $35,800. Any taxable income over $35,800 is taxed at the marginal rate.

In this example, the taxable income is $38,100. We have an amount of $38,100 - $35,800 = $2,300 taxable at 28 percent.

Mr. & Mrs. Investor pay a lower rate of 15 percent on the first $35,800 of taxable income $5,370 / 35,800 = 0.15.

Taxes owed on 28 percent marginal rate dollars = $2,300 x 28% = $644.

Their total tax liability is ($5,370 + $644) = $6,014.

They only paid 12 percent ($6,014 / $50,000 = 0.12) of earned income in taxes. They paid 15.8 percent ($6,014 / $38,100 = 0.158) of taxable income in taxes.

If their income rose $2,000 to $52,000, then they would pay taxes at the 28 percent rate on the $2,000 dollars which would be another $560 in taxes. This would increase their taxes to 16.4 percent from 15.8 percent of taxable income.

As you can see, for each additional dollar earned you pay taxes at the 28 percent rate. This is what is referred to as the marginal tax rate. It is the rate you pay for each additional dollar earned. Keep this idea in mind as you make investment decisions. If you can defer paying 28 percent of a portion of your earned income in taxes you have found a powerful wealth building tool.

Two excellent tax deferred investments are your company 401(k) plan and Individual Retirement Arrangements (IRA). Both of these investments allow you to defer some of your salary and they give you a tax break by lowering your taxable income. There are, of course, limitations to how much you can defer in these vehicles.

Be careful you don't spend all your time as an investor trying to avoid paying taxes. You may miss the real opportunity of other investments by getting into exotic and costly tax avoidance investments. While these types of investments may save you money in taxes you will end up losing money overall if they under perform and overcharge. Remember, it may be better to pay taxes and have a return on investments than to have no return at all.

Some popular tax avoidance investments that overcharge and under perform are limited partnerships and variable annuities.

Risk

Webster's dictionary defines **risk** as the chance that some *unfavorable* event will occur. Risk is a part of every aspect of our lives. We take the riskiness of some situations for granted because we become comfortable with them. As humans, we tend to fear the unknown.

You take risks every day. Every time you get into the car you are risking an auto accident. Thousands of people lose their lives each year in automobile accidents, but most of us do not think about how risky it is to drive. We become comfortable with driving because we are familiar with it and have experience doing it. We also must do it to maintain our life-style!

Once we have become familiar with the unknown we tend not to think of it as being risky.

In the realm of investing, the concept of risk is simple. To obtain a higher investment return you must be willing to take a greater risk. A good definition for **Investment risk** is the possibility that your original investment may be worth less after some given time period.

Risk is often difficult to understand and even more difficult to define and measure. Much work has been performed in this area. There are many different types of risk. Our discussion will focus on the risk associated with stocks, bonds and cash equivalents.

Loss of principle and loss of purchasing power are commonly associated with risk. **Loss of principle** is when your ending investment value is less than what you put into the investment. If you invest $1,000 and after one year your investment is only worth $900, you have lost $100 in principle. This is probably the most known and feared aspect of risk.

Loss of purchasing power is when the purchasing power of your investment is less after some period of time, even though the principle is preserved. For example, your $1,000 investment may have grown to $1,050, but inflation has pushed the real dollar value to $1,100 in the same time period. This means you need $1,100 to purchase the same goods and services as the $1,000 would have bought when the initial investment was made. Since your investment value only grew to $1,050, you have lost $50. Your total investment value is greater than when you started, but your purchasing ability has decreased.

Systematic Risk

Risk can be divided into two categories, *systematic* and *unsystematic*. **Systematic risk** is the general risk common to all investments and assumed by all investors. It is not unique to any investment vehicle. Included in systematic risk is inflation, interest rate and market risk.

Inflation risk is the possibility that an investment's performance will decline due to an increase in inflation. As explained earlier, inflation destroys the real dollar value of your investment. Although your investment may grow in value, you can not buy as much as you could have when you made the original investment. In other words, you have lost purchasing power. This is the "invisible" risk that creeps up on all investors.

Interest rate risk plays a major role in the outcome of your investment. A rise in interest rates depresses the market value of fixed income investments.

Market risk is the possibility that the entire financial market will decline. This happens when negative investor sentiment drives down the entire market even though assets are still strong. Wars, international conflicts and natural disasters have an adverse affect on financial markets. You probably have seen the stock market rise and fall on reports of bad news or just on rumors. The bond market tumbles every time the words *interest rate increase* are heard.

Unsystematic Risk

Unsystematic risk represents the portion of an investment's risk that can be eliminated through diversification. It results from uncontrollable or random events, such as labor strikes, lawsuits, loss of a major contract and regulatory actions. It affects various investment vehicles differently. Industry and company risk are types of unsystematic risk.

Industry risk is the possibility that an industry suffers a setback or declines. The great American steel industry suffered a major setback due to foreign competition and has never recovered.

There are many cyclical industries. During 1990 problems of savings and loan banks made the headlines. The financial industry was suffering a setback and their stock prices were deflated. A couple years later, financial stocks took off and became the hottest industry.

An industry may even collapse. Stock in the buggy whip industry would have been a bad investment during the Model-T era.

Company risk is the possibility that a company suffers a setback or goes out of business. Small, start-up companies come and go. Medium to large size companies tend to become more stable, however any size company may suffer a set back and go out of business. Remember Pan Am and Eastern Airlines?

The Risk & Return Trade-Off

As an investor, you are faced with a trade-off between the risk and the return of an investment. To obtain a higher investment return, you must be willing to take a greater risk. Figure 3.4 shows where most investments fall on the risk/return continuum.

As you move up the pyramid, the investments have a higher return potential but your principle is at greater risk. As you move down the pyramid, you reduce the risk of losing principle, but you also lower your investment return.

The lowest tier contains investments that are safe with regard to maintaining principle. These investments typically run at, or below the inflation rate. The middle tier shows growth investments. Their returns are typically above the inflation rate with less risk of principle than the top tier. The top tier contains investments with the highest risk, highest potential return. These investments are considered speculative and are extremely risky.

How to Reduce Risk By Diversifying

Risk can be reduced by **diversifying** or by spreading investment monies among several investment opportunities. By spreading your money, you are reducing the random risk that any one of your investments will go down in value. When you diversify, your rate of return will be higher than some of your individual investment returns and lower than others.
The key to diversification is "don't put all your eggs in one basket". There is more to diversification than just spreading your money around. This idea will be discussed further in the sections on stock and bond investing.

Figure 3.4   Risk Return Trade-Off

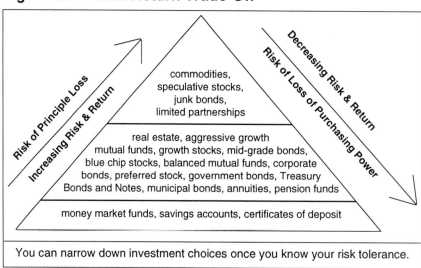

How To Build Wealth With Your 401(k)

Chapter 4

The Heart of Investing

There are seven categories of investments: stocks, bonds, cash equivalents, precious metals, commodities, collectibles, and real estate. See Table 4.1 for examples. There are also many ways to package and market these investments, i.e. IRA's, limited partnerships, life insurance and mutual funds. See Table 4.2.

Although there are several categories of investments, three are considered the basics: stocks, bonds and cash equivalents. Stocks represent ownership of a company. Because you are an owner, you are entitled to share in both the company's profits and it's losses. Bonds are debt obligations. As a bond owner, you charge a fixed interest for lending your money to a

With most 401(k) plans you invest via mutual funds which are typically invested in stocks, bonds and cash equivalents.

Table 4.1   **Investment Types**

Investment Type	Examples
stocks	common stock, preferred stock, blue chips, cyclical
bonds	treasury notes, bonds, municipal, corporate, junk
cash equivalents	treasury bills, commercial paper
precious metals	gold, silver, platinum
commodities	everything from pork bellies to soybeans, to financial futures
collectibles	art, china, baseball cards
real estate	apartments, single family homes, land
There's an investment that matches almost any interest and risk tolerance.	

Table 4.2   **Investment Packages**

Investment Package	Examples
mutual funds	open end, closed end, stocks, bonds, money market, mixture
IRA's	stocks, bonds, mutual funds
life insurance	annuities, whole life insurance, variable annuities
limited partnerships	real estate, business ventures
Not only are there different types of investments, but they can also be packaged into different formats.	

borrower. The borrower can be a company or a government agency. Bonds are typically a long term obligation. Cash equivalents are securities that can be transferred to cash in a short period of time with virtually no risk to the principle. Examples include treasury bills, negotiable certificates of deposit, and corporate short term notes. Money market funds are composed of cash equivalents.

What You Need to Know About Stocks

Stocks are shares of ownership in a company. Companies sell stock to raise money. Investors buy stocks to make money. There are two ways to make money from stock ownership: dividends and capital appreciation. **Dividends** are paid when a company is doing well and distributes a portion of profits to its owners. It is a cash distribution. **Capital appreciation** is when the market value of a stock goes up. **Market value** (or **market price**) is the current price a buyer is willing to pay a seller. A stock's price generally goes up when the company is doing well.

Types of Stock

Common stock is the most basic form of ownership of a corporation. If you own stock, you are called a **stockholder** or **shareholder**. As an owner, you have a claim on company assets, but only after bondholders and preferred stockholders

60

(discussed later) have been paid. The revenues of a company generally are used to pay expenses, interest to bondholders, taxes, cash dividends to preferred stockholders and cash dividends to common stockholders, in that order. Of course some revenues are retained to fuel company growth. A company may have one stockholder or thousands of stockholders and you can own more than one share of stock. The more shares you own, the greater your ownership rights.

When we talk about common stocks we sometimes use the term **equities**. Equity is simply the difference between the value of a company's assets minus its liabilities. As a shareholder your claim is on the equity of the company. It is much like ownership of a house. If a house is worth $100,000 and there is a mortgage loan of $75,000, then the equity in the house is $25,000. As the owner of the house you are entitled to the $25,000 in equity.

As a shareholder you also have a say in how the company is run. You vote for a board of directors and the board of directors hires a management team to run the company. Issues relating to the company are voted on at the stockholders annual meeting. You typically have one vote for each share you own. The total number of votes is equal to the total number of outstanding shares. You can assign your votes to the board of directors by proxy. Many shareholders vote by proxy.

Stocks are sold to individual investors through brokers who trade on one of the stock exchanges. The largest and best known exchange is the New York Stock Exchange (NYSE). The other major exchanges are the American Stock Exchange (AMEX), and the Over-The-Counter market (OTC). A subset of the OTC market is the National Association of Dealers Automated Quotation (NASDAQ). See Table 4.3 for a description of the exchanges.

Preferred stock is somewhat of a cross between a bond and a common stock. Like a bond, it is a fixed-income security because it receives a fixed dividend rate. Like a stock, it represents ownership in the company. The owner of a preferred stock does not share in any extra profits made by the company because the dividend rate is fixed. On the other hand, if the company does poorly, the preferred stock owner is

Table 4.3   Major U.S. Stock Exchanges

Exchange	Stocks Listed	Type of Companies	Requirements
NYSE	Over 2,000	Larger, established, well-known companies	1.1 million outstanding shares. A market value of $18 million.
AMEX	Over 800	Mid- to small-size companies	500,000 outstanding shares. Assets of $4 million.
OTC	Over 30,000	Typically small companies. Some large companies have stayed on the OTC.	Minimum

The NYSE, AMEX and OTC are the largest exchanges. There are also several regional exchanges.

entitled to payment before the common stockholder. The price of preferred stock moves more slowly than common stock and is influenced by interest rates. Preferred stockholders usually do not have voting privileges.

Stocks can be categorized by market size which is determined by the company's market capitalization. **Market capitalization** is a single share price multiplied by the number of outstanding shares. There is no clear cut definition of a small, medium or large capitalization stock, but I'll explain some general guidelines.

Small cap (short for capitalization) companies are referred to as emerging companies, shadow stocks or just plain small stocks. These companies are starting up and have little profitability. They reinvest all profits back into the company and usually don't pay dividends. These stocks are favored for high growth. They also contain the greatest risk. Small capitalization values may be from $0 to $500 million.

Mid cap companies are typically more established and have a track record of growth and earnings. They typically pay little or no dividends because the company needs to retain money for growth. Mid caps are considered by some investors to be the best positioned stock as categorized by size. They are more established and less risky than small caps and more flexible and faster growing than the large caps. The mid cap values are generally between $500 million and $1 billion.

How To Build Wealth With Your 401(k)

Large caps represent well-established companies. They own a large share of the market and typically have a good track record of earnings and growth. Large caps generally have capitalization values in excess of $1 billion.

There are more detailed ways to classify a stock than by size. Stocks can also be categorized as income, growth, blue chip, speculative or cyclical.

Income stocks typically pay a large dividend to shareholders. They usually represent well-established companies with good earnings. The representative market share is stable and competition is minimal. Utility stocks are typically considered income stocks. Income stocks are preferred by investors who seek current income and who are less interested in capital gains.

Growth stocks typically pay little or no dividends. Company profits are reinvested into the corporation to keep the company growing. Growth is needed to increase market share and profitability which in turn increases the value of the stock. Growth stock investors expect to profit through capital gains. Growth companies are typically small to mid sized with expanding product lines and growing markets. Some examples of growth stocks are Wal-Mart, Home Depot, Rubbermaid and The Gap. This type of stock is good for those who desire high rates of returns over many years and who are less interested in current income.

Blue chip stocks are a cross between growth and income stocks. They represent large, well-established corporations with a long and stable history of earnings and dividend payouts. These corporations are the leaders in their industry and usually set the standards for other companies. A few commonly known blue chip stocks are McDonald's, General Electric, Merck, AT&T and Dun & Bradstreet. Companies considered to be blue chips in the early part of this decade are not necessarily still in the same category today. A blue chip company today may not be in business ten years from now. Blue Chip stocks are bought by investors who want current income, price appreciation and the security of investing in a stable company.

Cyclical stocks are those that rise and fall with economic conditions. When times are good, these stocks generally increase. When the economy is bad, the value of these stocks typically goes down. Some cyclical stocks rise and fall inversely to economic conditions. In other words, when the economy does well this type of stock does poorly. When the economy falls, an inversely performing cyclical will increase in value. The most well-known cyclical industries are airlines, auto manufacturers and paper and steel mills. These stocks are bought by investors who feel the economy will change in a direction that will increase the stock's price.

Speculative stocks, also known as **penny stocks**, are stocks in new, untested companies selling for a dollar or two per share. Most of these companies fail. These are the smallest of small company stocks. They are usually start-up companies that have yet to establish their product in the market. With penny stocks, you have great potential for high returns. As a result, the risk is extremely high. Investors who play with the speculative stocks are going for the home run and are willing to take a strike out.

How to Measure Stock Risk

By now you probably realize that a good understanding of risk is important to the success of your stock investment. You already know what risk is and have been introduced to several different types. Now let's talk about how it can be measured.

The most common way to measure the relative riskiness of a stock is by its beta. **Beta** is a statistical measure of a stock's price volatility in relation to the overall market as measured by the S&P 500. The **S&P 500** is a market index consisting of 500 stocks that represent the stock market as a whole.

Any stock that has at least a three year track record has a calculated beta. A stock's beta is determined by comparing its historical performance to the performance of the stock market as a whole. A stock's individual beta indicates its performance variation relative to the entire market.

Beta's can be positive or negative. A positive beta means the stock moves in the same direction as the market. A negative beta means that the stock moves in the opposite direction. Most betas are positive.

Stocks that move in step with the market as measured by the Standard and Poor 500 have a beta of one. Stocks that are more volatile than the market have a beta greater then one. Stocks that are less volatile then the market have a beta less than one. Most stocks have a beta between +0.5 and +2.0. Figure 4.1 compares the performance of a stock with a beta greater than one to a stock with a beta less than one.

Stocks in general tend to move up and down with the market. Some stocks move much faster, while others move slower.

A second way to measure the relative riskiness of a stock is by its alpha. **Alpha** is a measure of the risk adjusted premium or deficit a stock has returned in relation to the S&P 500 index. A positive alpha indicates that the stock has a higher risk adjusted return than the market. A negative alpha indicates that the stock has a lower risk adjusted return than the market.

Beta tells you if a stock has a history of being more or less volatile than the market. Alpha indicates if the stock has returned a premium or deficit in return for the same time period. As an investor, you want to keep your beta's low and your alpha's high. Now that you know how to measure risk, let's talk about techniques to reduce it.

Stock Diversification

Stock diversification is the process of spreading your stock portfolio among stocks from different companies and different industries. This prevents a total disaster if one company or an entire industry collapse. Diversification can reduce and practically eliminate unsystematic risk. Remember that unsystematic risk is the risk that affects investment types differently. A good example is when an entire industry or company collapses. Systematic risk is the general risk common to all investments such as inflation, market conditions and interest rates.

Figure 4.1   Stock Performance Measurement Using Beta

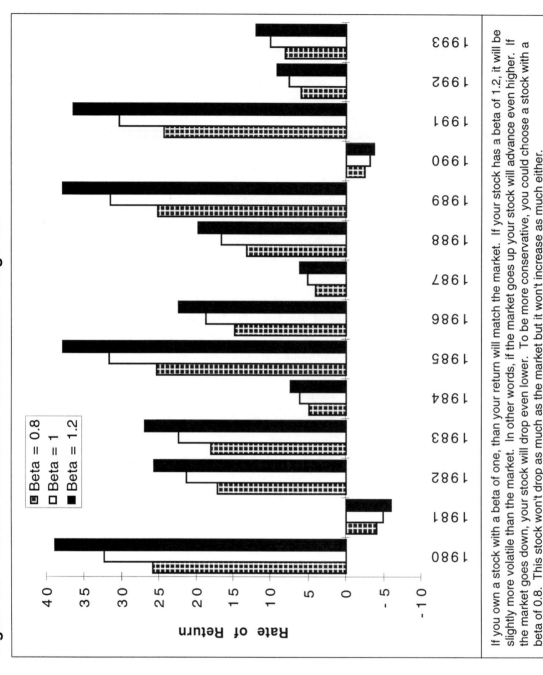

If you own a stock with a beta of one, than your return will match the market. If your stock has a beta of 1.2, it will be slightly more volatile than the market. In other words, if the market goes up your stock will advance even higher. If the market goes down, your stock will drop even lower. To be more conservative, you could choose a stock with a beta of 0.8. This stock won't drop as much as the market but it won't increase as much either.

How To Build Wealth With Your 401(k)

An example of a well diversified portfolio of stocks would be one that contains General Electric, Ford Motor Co., Bristol Myers, Wal-Mart, General Foods and Duracell International. This portfolio is subject only to systematic risk.

A poorly diversified portfolio would be one holding stocks in only one or two industries. A portfolio containing General Motors, Ford and Chrysler Corp. is an example of an undiversified portfolio. This portfolio is subject to both systematic risk and unsystematic risk.

Because unsystematic risk can be virtually eliminated through diversification, you need only worry about systematic risk. In the case of stocks, this is predominantly market risk. In general, a falling market will have a negative effect on most stocks. You cannot control or diversify systematic risk.

If you tend to be a moderate investor, you could build a portfolio that resembles the S&P 500. In this case, your beta is one. If you want to achieve a higher return and are willing to take on additional risk, you could build a portfolio with a beta greater than one. Conservative investors stick to betas of less than one.

What You Need to Know About Bonds

As mentioned earlier, bonds are debt obligations. As a bond owner, you charge a fixed interest for lending your money to a borrower. The borrower can be a company, municipality or a government agency. The bond is either backed by assets or by the full faith of the issuing organization.

A bond is essentially an IOU.

Types of Bonds

U.S. Government securities fall into two general categories: (1) Treasury bills, notes and bonds, and (2) Agency issue notes, bonds and certificates. Treasury Bills, known as T-Bills have maturities of 13 to 52 weeks. They are used by the Federal Reserve to control the money supply. Notes have maturities of 2 to 10 years and serve to finance projects.

Long-term treasury bonds have maturities of 30 years and are used to finance long-term debt.

Corporate bonds are issued by corporations. They have short, intermediate and long maturity lengths. They are considered more risky than government bonds and offer a higher rate of return. **Junk bonds** are also issued by corporations but these issuers have little to no ability to repay their debt. Junk bonds offer a high rate of return and are very risky.

Local governments issue **municipal bonds**, called munis, to finance local projects. Munis are given special tax consideration to attract investors. They are usually exempt from federal, state and local income taxes and offer a lower rate of return because of the tax advantages. Munis can be of two basic types, revenue or general obligation bonds. Revenue bonds are backed by the revenues generated by the project. General obligation bonds are backed by property taxes.

How Bonds Make and Lose Money

The **face value** of a bond represents its original issue price. **Maturity date** is when the bond is retired or paid off. At this time the face value of the bond is returned to the owner. The **interest rate** is the amount of interest paid to the bond holder. It is fixed and paid at set intervals. The intended life of a bond, or its maturity length, is generally classified as short-, intermediate- or long- term. Interest rates are usually higher for longer term bonds.

When you buy a bond, you receive a fixed rate of return until maturity. When the bond is retired, the bond owner is paid the face value of that bond. Although the interest rate on a bond is fixed, its market value is not. Bonds are bought and sold many times before they reach maturity. When the bond is sold, its market price is determined by the prevailing interest rates at that time. If you are trying to sell a bond with a rate of 5 percent and similar investments are yielding 7 percent, you will have a hard time selling that bond unless you reduce its price. This is why bond prices fall when interest rates rise and increase when they drop.

How To Build Wealth With Your 401(k)

Let's use an example to understand this better. Suppose the prevailing interest rate is 10 percent for a 15 year bond. You pay the face value of $1,000 and receive a bond that will pay you 10 percent interest per year for 15 years. If you hold the bond to its maturity, you will get the face value of $1,000 back along with $100 per year interest payments for the 15 years.

After one year, the interest rate on the same type of 15 year bond rises to 15 percent. You are now stuck with a bond that pays only 10 percent for the next 14 years while your annoying friend keeps telling you how he bought the same type of bond that is now paying 15 percent.

Mad, and maybe embarrassed, you head downtown to sell your bond. Unfortunately, nobody will pay you $1,000 dollars for a bond that only earns 10 percent. At least not when they can get one that earns 15 percent. Really mad you start home. As you get to your car someone from behind the building offers to buy your bond. Wait, he wants a discounted price! Yes, if you want to unload a lower interest paying bond than you better discount it. The going price for a 10 percent bond while others are 15 percent is $713.40. To sell your bond you must discount it to a point where it will provide a total yield of around 15 percent. (There is a formula but let's leave this one for the calculator!)

The one year return on your bond investment is -18.66 percent. It is equal to the $100 interest plus the lower value of your bond. The value of your bond dropped to 28.66 percent lower than the purchase price. This is why your return is negative.

Yes, if you hold your bond to maturity you will get your $1,000 back plus 10 percent interest but this has a big down-fall. You will be stuck listening to your friend brag about his bond earning 15 percent for an entire 14 years! *If you hold your bond to maturity you lose the opportunity to earn a 5 percent higher rate of return.*

Now let's look at it from a falling interest rate perspective. If interest rates fall to 5 percent for bonds, you will probably be the person behind the building trying to sell your 10 percent bond but this time at a premium. The value of your bond will be $1,494.90 (same calculator). If you sell this bond you will make a nice little profit of $594.90 after one year. Your profit is made up of the $494.90 premium plus the $100 interest earned for the one year. Your total return is 59.5 percent. This is how bond funds make big money.

In reality, many other considerations are taken into account when buying or selling a bond. Many bond investors do not hold their bonds until maturity. The interest fluctuations are used to create capital gains by buying and selling bonds before maturity. Many bond investors use funds to invest in bonds.

Interest rate fluctuations play a major role in bond fund performance. Bonds are sold when rates change as little as 1/4 percent. When rates drop, bond funds reap gains. When they increase, the bond returns are lower. A bond fund can produce negative results. If you get caught with low interest rate bonds in a time of continually rising interest rates you could lose, and lose big.

Table 4.4 shows how the value of your bond increases and decreases when prevailing interest rates change. The example shows a $1,000 bond with a 10 percent interest rate and a 15 year maturity. The bond maintains it's $1,000 value as long as market interest rates remain the same. When market rates fall, the bond's value increases. Notice that the further away from maturity, the greater the premium placed on the bond value. You can also see that when market rates increase, the value of the bond decreases.

Table 4.4   Bond Value Fluctuations Due To Interest Rates

| Market Rate | Years after bond issued | | | | |
	1	2	3	4	5
5.00%	$1,494.93	$1,469.68	$1,443.16	$1,415.32	$1,386.09
10.00%	$1,000.00	$1,000.00	$1,000.00	$1,000.00	$1,000.00
15.00%	$713.78	$720.84	$728.97	$738.31	$770.56
20.00%	$538.94	$546.73	$556.08	$567.29	$580.75

Although the interest paid on a bond is fixed, its price is not. When interest rates increase, the value of your bond decreases. This Illustration is for a $1,000 bond with a 15 year maturity and 10% interest rate.

Bond Risk

The risk associated with bonds is predominately interest rate risk, inflation risk and credit risk. Interest rate risk is systematic risk and can not be avoided. Although the *relationship* between bonds and interest rates is known (when interest rates rise, bonds values fall), there is no way to predict what the exact interest rate will be. Inflation risk is also systematic risk and can not be avoided. When bonds are initially issued, the current rate of inflation is taken into account, but if inflation grows, the bond's value is diminished. Although you receive your principle back at maturity, it may be worth very little in real dollars. Long-term bonds are more susceptible to the risk of inflation and interest rate. Intermediate bonds are less sensitive to interest rate variations and inflation but offer lower interest rates. See Table 4.5.

Bond holders also have to contend with credit risk which is the risk that a company can not repay its debt. If a troubled company is unable to pay, you may lose all or part of your investment. When a company defaults or goes bankrupt, creditors have to take what they can get. Sometimes it's pennies on the dollar. Government bonds are backed by the full faith of the U.S. government. As a result, they are considered the safest. Municipal bonds are backed by local governments and can default. Corporate bonds are backed by the

Table 4.5   Sensitivity Of Long-Term Bonds

Market Rate	2-Year Bond	15-Year Bond	30-Year Bond
5.00%	$1,047.62	$1,494.93	$1,757.05
10.00%	$1,000.00	$1,000.00	$1,000.00
15.00%	$956.52	$713.78	$672.46
20.00%	$916.67	$538.94	$502.53

Notice how the price of the 30-year bond drops more drastically when interest rates increase than does the two year bond. This table shows the sensitivity of different term bond values one year after issue. In this example, all bonds are $1,000 and have a rate of 10 percent.

corporation's ability to pay and may be subject to default if the company fails. There are several independent firms that rate corporate and municipal bonds. Moody's and Standard & Poor's are the leading evaluators. U.S. Government bonds are not rated.

Moody's and Standard & Poor's use different symbols to rate bonds. Their ratings are not a recommendation of which bonds to buy and sell. Rather they are intended to provide an independent assessment of the credit worthiness of the issuer. Standard and Poor's rating system uses "AAA" to mean the highest rating and lowest risk, and a "CCC" represents the lowest rating and highest risk. Ratings are assigned in between. An "AAA" rated bond is the highest and an "AA" is the next level. A single "A" rating would be below "AA" but above "BBB". The process continues to a single "C" rating being the lowest. See Table 4.6 for a comparison of Standard & Poor's rating system to Moody's rating system. "BBB" rated bonds and higher are usually referred to as investment grade bonds. The lower rated bonds are usually referred to as speculative with the lowest rated referred to as junk bonds.

A bond that is rated higher and considered less risky can be issued at a lower interest rate. Remember an investor will accept a lower rate for a less risky investment. Of course, low rated bonds have a higher interest rate because investors demand a higher rate of return for a riskier investment.

Bond Diversification

Credit risk is unsystematic, meaning that it can be diversified away. Remember that interest rate risk and inflation risk are common to all investors and can not be avoided. Diversification practically eliminates credit risk. The object is to buy bonds from different companies and across different industries.

To create an investment grade, corporate bond portfolio you would invest in company bonds rated AA or better that represent companies from different industries. To achieve higher yields, you could add speculative graded bonds to your portfolio which would give you higher returns with a slightly higher risk. This portfolio is not as risky as one made up entirely of speculative bonds.

How To Build Wealth With Your 401(k)

A process called **chaining**, or **laddering** can limit your exposure to interest rate and inflation risk. Chaining is when you buy bonds with different maturities. This means your bonds will come due at different times. As a result, you limit the risk of having all your bonds come due during a low interest rate period.

Bond funds operate using the chaining technique. A fund investing in intermediate bonds is continually buying and selling bonds of different intermediate maturities. The long-term performance of a bond fund will usually track the average performance of the type of bonds it is investing in. Bond funds measure risk by the average weighted maturity. The longer the maturity length of the portfolio, the more sensitive (risky) the portfolio is to interest rate changes. Let's recap how bonds work.

Table 4.6   Bond Rating Systems

Standard & Poor	Moody's	Definition
AAA	Aaa	Highest investment grade issue
AA	Aa	High grade investment issue
A	A	Medium grade investment issue
BBB	Baa	Lowest investment grade rating
BB	Ba	Speculative grade issue
B	B	Speculative grade issue
CCC	Caa	Junk bonds, poor quality issue
CC	Ca	Junk bonds, very poor quality
C	C	Junk bonds, probable default
CI		Suspended interest payments
D		Defaulted
Comparison of the two most widely used bond rating systems.		

- Bonds pay a fixed interest rate determined when the bond is issued.
- Bond values fluctuate with interest rates.
- If interest rates increase, bond values decrease.
- If interest rates decrease, bond values increase.
- Bonds held to maturity will return the face value of the bond regardless of interest rate fluctuations during the years.

Fundamentals of Cash Equivalents

Cash equivalents are assets that can be turned into cash quickly. They have a maturity of less than one year and are easily sold at any time. Examples include Treasury Bills issued by the Federal Reserve and commercial paper generated by companies needing short-term loans of several days to months.

Cash equivalents usually have a rate of return close to the prevailing inflation rate. They are short-term investments used to protect the real dollar value of your money by returning a rate of return close to the inflation rate. They are usually sold in large sums and are not typically available to individual investors. Cash equivalents are sold in what is called the **money market**. Long and intermediate bonds are sold in the **capital market**.

Individual investor's desire to invest in cash equivalents lead to the creation of money market funds. **Money market funds** allow investors to pool their money and invest in a form of cash equivalents that produce better returns than savings account or certificates of deposit. A money market fund *is not* federally insured as a bank savings account or certificate of deposit. However, money market funds are considered very safe.

When to Buy Stocks, Bonds, and Cash Equivalents

Stocks allow you to invest for maximum capital appreciation, current income or a combination of both. Stocks are very attractive for long-term investing because they allow you to keep ahead of inflation and reap the rewards of profitable companies. There is theoretically no fixed limit on the amount you can earn by investing in stocks, but you must be willing to hang in for the long haul. By adopting a long-term attitude, you lessen your worries when the market goes down and you are able to recruit the power of compound interest to your advantage.

Investors buy bonds to receive a fixed current income and to preserve principle. Bonds pay a higher current income than most stocks. Unlike stocks, bonds cannot reduce or suspend interest payments unless they default. And, there is a fixed ceiling on the amount you can earn when buying a bond because you are not sharing in company profits as you do with stocks.

Cash equivalents are used by investors as a short-term holding vehicle. The money market allows you to earn the rate of inflation and not lose purchasing power. Of course the return is small.

How To Build Wealth With Your 401(k)

Chapter 5

The Best Way to Evaluate Investment Performance

You've heard of the Dow Jones Industrial Average, but have you heard of the Wilshire 5000? Both of these are market indexes. **Market indexes,** or averages, are used to measure the general behavior of an asset class. There are different indexes associated with different asset classes. The indexes tend to gauge either a broad range of the asset class or specific areas.

Benchmarking

Indexes are a measuring tool you can use to judge the performance of your portfolio. This process is called **benchmarking**. For example, let's say you have an investment that seems to be performing poorly. To find out for sure, you can compare it to the appropriate index. If your investment has a higher return than the index it is actually doing well for that asset class. The opposite is also true. If your investment under performs the matching index then you know it is not doing well.

Although helpful, indexes are not perfect. Different indexes for the same type of asset class may have different performance numbers because they use different methods to arrive at their values. Major indexes are listed in newspapers and broadcasted on TV and radio.

Stock Market Indicators

Stock market indexes tend to gauge either the performance of the market as a whole, or the performance of specific portions such as small or industrial stocks. Because stock indexes use different methods to calculate performance, they are typically quoted as a percent change. This is the method we will use in our discussion. There are several well known indexes: the Dow Jones Industrial Average, the Standard and Poor 500, and the NASDAQ composite.

The original and most widely quoted stock market indicator is the **Dow Jones Industrial Average** (DJIA). This index contains 30 leading industrial stocks that are believed to represent the overall market. The stocks that make up the DJIA change from time to time as the companies in the index fall out of favor and others grow more popular. See Table 5.1 for a list of the 1992 Dow Jones Industrial companies.

Dow Jones has four other indexes that represent specific areas of the stock market: the Transportation Average, the Utility Average, the Dow Jones Composite and the Worldwide Aver-

Table 5.1   Dow Jones Industrial Companies

Goodyear	Bethlehem Steel	Du Pont
Merck	Caterpillar	Union Carbide
Coca Cola	Woolworth	Exxon
Allied-Signal	Texaco	Eastman Kodak
Phillip Morris	General Motors	United Tech
J.P. Morgan	IBM	Disney
Sears Roebuck	Westinghouse	Alcoa
General Electric	AT&T	Minnesota Mining
International Paper	Boeing	Procter & Gamble
McDonald's	Chevron	American Express

These 30 companies are the Dow Jones Industrials as of 1992.

age. The **Transportation Average** is made up of 20 stocks which include railroad, trucking, and airline companies. The **Utility Average** is made up of 15 utility stocks. The Dow Jones **Composite** is composed of these two plus the DJIA and contains 65 stocks all together. The Dow Jones **Worldwide Average** was created in response to the increasing interest in overseas markets. It was started in 1993 and is designed to gauge the performance of the world's markets. It is broken down by countries.

The DJIA was a good indicator of overall stock performance at the turn of the century. At that time, industrial companies represented the growth of the country. Because the economy has changed, the S&P 500 index is now considered to represent the overall stock market performance better.

The **S&P 500 index** is a composite of four other S&P indexes; industrials, transportation, utilities, and financials. The **industrials** contain 400 stocks. The **transportation** index contains 20 stocks. The **utilities** index contains 40 stocks. And the **financial index** also contains 40 stocks. The S&P 500 contains more stocks than the DJIA. It is a broad based stock market indicator that represents about 80 percent of the total market value. Stocks in the S&P 500 are weighted according to their relative market value. This way stocks are better represented according to their importance in the market.

The S&P 500 is probably the most widely used benchmark for measuring stock market performance, although the DJIA is the most quoted.

All three major exchanges have indexes. They are the **New York Stock Exchange** (NYSE), the **National Association of Securities Dealers Automated Quotation** (NASDAQ), and the **American Stock Exchange** (AMEX). The NYSE index contains all the stocks listed on the exchange which is over 2,000 different stocks. The AMEX index also contains all the stocks traded on its exchange which is about 900 stocks. The NASDAQ indexes track the performance of thousands of stocks traded in the over the counter market (OTC). The NASDAQ composite is the most often quoted NASDAQ index and reflects the performance of over 4,000 stocks traded on the NASDAQ.

The NASDAQ composite is often used as the benchmark for small stock performance.

The **Wilshire 5000** represents the total dollar value of 5,000 stocks traded on the NYSE, AMEX, and NASDAQ. Unlike individual stock exchanges, the Wilshire is a broad-based index and measures stock performance across the market.

Value Line is a stock research company that publishes their own averages. The **Value Line Composite Average** contains about 1,700 stocks tracked across the NYSE, NASDAQ and AMEX exchanges. This index is similar to the Wilshire 5000.

The fast growing popularity of foreign country mutual fund investing has influenced some 401(k) plans to offer these types of funds to plan participants. International funds offer investors more diversification and an opportunity to invest in financial markets broader than just the United States. Foreign market indexes allow investors to measure how the other financial markets are performing. If you are investing in a mutual fund that has most of its assets in foreign countries, then you would need to use the foreign market indexes to gauge its performance.

There are some foreign indexes that have been around longer than the Dow Jones World Index and that are more popular. **Morgan Stanley Foreign Indexes** measures the foreign market performance by individual regions or as a broader measure of several regions. The most popular Morgan Stanley Foreign Indexes are the **World Equities Market Index**, and the **Morgan Stanley Europe Australia and Far East (MSCIEAFE) Index**. The MSCIEAFE is widely used to gauge the overall foreign stock market movement, similar to the S&P 500 which measures U.S. market movement. If you have an international or worldwide fund, this index will help gauge performance. If you have a foreign fund that invests in a particular region, than you would be better off with an index that only measures that region.

Because of the advanced use of computers, many companies are now publishing their own averages. Differences sometimes exist between indexes in the same class because different calculation methods are used.

When comparing indexes or assets to indexes you must be sure that the start and end dates relating to investment return are the same.

If you are comparing the yearly performance of an asset for the period ending Dec. 31, then you must use an index with the yearly period ending Dec. 31. If the periods are off by as little as one month, your comparison could be very misleading because the market changes frequently.

There are two ways an index represents performance; capital appreciation or total return. Total return is capital appreciation plus dividend reinvestment. It is usually calculated on a quarterly or yearly basis. Indexes quoted on TV and in the paper are usually based on capital appreciation. This shows the growth of an asset, but does not take into account the dividends. Figure 5.1 shows the difference in growth between total return and capital appreciation. It is best to compare investments, especially long-term investments by their total return because you can then take into account the full power of compound interest.

Mutual funds report their performance as total return. You should use indexes that show total return when comparing performance.

The index considered best for tracking mid to large stocks traded on the NYSE is the S&P 500. The index considered best to track small or OTC stocks is the NASDAQ composite.

Bond Market Indicators

There are several bond indicators available. Most are handled by investment institutions such as Morgan Stanley, Lehman Brothers, and Soloman Brothers. There is also a Dow Jones bond average and a rating system called Bond Buyer.

Because bonds are not heavily traded by individual investors, there has never been a need for numerous bond indicators. The ones that do exist are usually categorized by bond type and by length of maturity. Examples of bond types are long-term corporate, intermediate corporate, short-term corporate,

Figure 5.1 Difference Between Total Return and Capital Appreciation

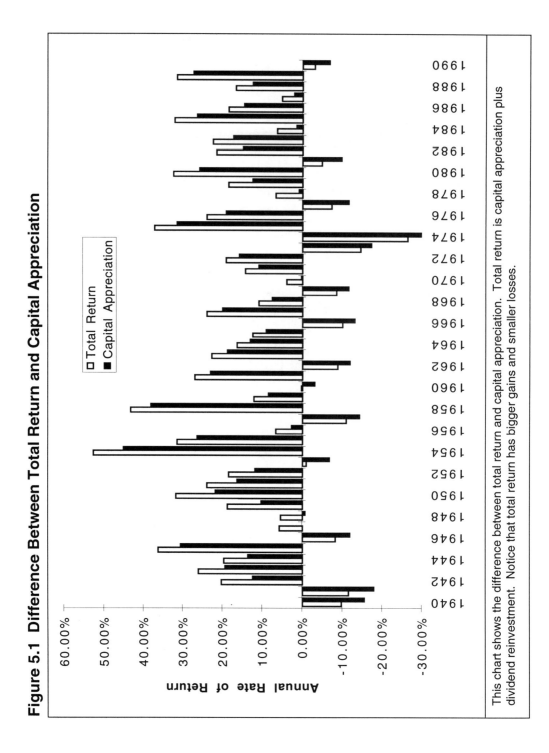

This chart shows the difference between total return and capital appreciation. Total return is capital appreciation plus dividend reinvestment. Notice that total return has bigger gains and smaller losses.

How To Build Wealth With Your 401(k)

Treasury Bills, intermediate government, long-term government, and municipal. Bond indicators typically give performance with respect to total return (interest income plus capital gains or losses). Morgan Stanley and Lehman Brothers track bond performance in many of the different categories. See Table 5.2 for a description of the Lehman Brothers Index.

Historical Investment Performance

By now you have gained a basic understanding of what stocks, bonds and cash equivalents are. Now is a good time to compare the returns you can expect from each of these investment classes. The best way to do this is to look at historical performances based on market indicators. Keep in mind that past performance does not guarantee future results but it does give

Table 5.2   **Lehman Brothers Bond Index Summary**

Lehman Brothers Index	Description
Aggregate Bond Index	Mix of corporate and government bonds with different maturities
Long-Term Government Bond Index	Government issued bonds with maturities of ten years or more
Intermediate-Term Government Bond Index	Government bonds with maturities of one to ten years
Long-Term Corporate Bond Index	Corporate issued, fixed-rate, non-convertible, investment grade bonds with maturities of ten years or more
Intermediate-Term Corporate Bond Index	Corporate issued fixed-rate, non-convertible, investment grade bonds with maturities of one to ten years
Intermediate-Term Treasury Index	U.S. Treasury issued debt with maturities of one to ten years
Long-Term Treasury Index	U.S. Treasury issued debt with maturities of ten or more years
Municipal Bond Index	Contains over 6,000 municipal bonds rated BAA or better with maturities of more than one year

us a way to compare performances between different investment types.

Table 5.3 shows a 60 year performance history of stocks, bonds, Treasury Bills and inflation. As you would expect, Treasury Bills just barely outperform inflation. Stocks and bonds have similar performances over a short period but stocks zoom past bonds in the long run. Table 5.3 also shows that small stocks have a better return than the S&P 500 when held for a long period and corporate bonds slightly outperform government bonds. You would expect this since you get a higher return in exchange for higher risk.

Table 5.4 shows the final value of $1 invested from 1934 to 1993 when different investment vehicles were used. The results are amazing. The dollar invested in small stocks grew to an impressive $4,618.70! In comparison, the dollar invested in corporate bonds grew to $24.84 and the dollar invested in Treasury Bills grew to $9.93. Treasury Bills didn't even keep pace with inflation. Table 5.4 clearly shows the power of compound interest over time and how small differences in interest rates can have a tremendous impact on the final value of your investment.

Stock Returns

Let's look at the annual return of the S&P 500 from 1941 to 1990. Remember that the S&P 500 is a market indicator that represents the stock market as a whole. Figure 5.2 shows the annual returns of the S&P 500 from 1941 to 1990. On the surface, you can see why an individual may fear the stock market. It posted negative returns 13 times during this 50 year period. But let's look at the big picture. The average annual return was 11.97 percent! How could you end up with such a good return when the market dropped 26 percent of the time? Because each drop was compensated for by very big gains. This is typical of the stock market. There will be losses from time to time, but there will also be large gains.

When the market drops it is called a **bear market**, or is said to be undergoing a **market correction**. If you ride out these corrections, you can end up with a substantial gain. Psychologically, this is difficult to do. When you see your invest-

Table 5.3   **60 Year Performance History**

1934-1993 In the Last...	S&P 500	Small Stocks	Long-Term Corporate Bonds	Long-Term Government Bonds	Treasury Bills	Inflation CPI
10 Years	14.90%	10.00%	14.00%	14.40%	6.40%	3.70%
20 Years	12.80%	18.80%	10.20%	10.10%	7.50%	5.90%
30 Years	10.50%	15.00%	10.20%	7.40%	6.70%	5.30%
40 Years	11.80%	15.40%	7.70%	6.00%	5.60%	4.30%
50 Years	12.30%	15.30%	6.40%	5.20%	4.60%	4.30%
60 Years	11.40%	15.10%	5.50%	5.10%	3.90%	4.10%

Source: Stocks, Bonds, Bills, and Inflation: 1993 Yearbook Ibbotson Associates, Inc., Chicago 1993.

This chart shows the 60 year performance history of stocks, bonds, and T-Bills. The last column shows the rate of inflation of the same period using the Consumer Price Index (CPI).

Chapter 5 / The Best Way to Evaluate Investment Performance   85

Table 5.4   One Dollar Invested In Different Vehicles

1934-1993 In the Last...	S&P 500	Small Stocks	Long-Term Corporate Bonds	Long-Term Government Bonds	Treasury Bills	Inflation CPI
10 Years	$4.01	$2.59	$3.71	$3.84	$1.86	$1.44
20 Years	$11.12	$31.36	$6.98	$6.85	$4.25	$3.15
30 Years	$19.99	$66.21	$9.26	$8.51	$7.00	$4.71
40 Years	$86.63	$307.77	$11.96	$10.29	$8.84	$5.39
50 Years	$330.36	$1,234.43	$15.25	$12.61	$9.48	$8.21
60 Years	$650.30	$4,618.70	$24.84	$19.78	$9.93	$11.14

Source: Stocks, Bonds, Bills, and Inflation: 1993 Yearbook; Ibbotson Associates, Inc., Chicago 1993

This chart shows the final value of one dollar when invested in different vehicles. Over the long run, small stocks far outpace bonds and T-Bills didn't even keep pace with inflation.

How To Build Wealth With Your 401(k)

ments drop 15 percent or more it makes you want to pull back and hide.

The two-year bear market of 1973 and 1974 equalled a 37.25 percent drop in cumulative market value. If you left the market during the down period, you would have lost a lot of money. If you stayed in the market, you would have gained back 37.14 percent the next year and an additional 23.81 percent in 1976. In fact, the five years after the 1973 / 1974 bear market showed an annual rate of return of almost 15 percent!

Now let's say you stayed in the market through 1990. What happened? The market dropped again in 1977, 1981, and 1990 but your average annual return stayed up at 14 percent! And what about Black Monday in 1987? Look closely at Figure 5.2; 1987 ended with a 5 percent gain!

The moral of the story is...

When you invest in the stock market, stay in for the long run!

Price variations in the market smooth out over a long period. Figure 5.3 shows market returns within five year periods from 1941 to 1990. This is called a rolling average. Notice how there is now only one year with a negative return.

Figure 5.4 shows a 10 year rolling average over the same 50 years. Now you can really see the effect of long-term investing; there are no market losses at all! Here are more words of wisdom...

In order to achieve higher returns, you must be willing to take larger risks and you must be able to ride out market fluctuations.

Stocks are suited for long-term investors. The longer your investment time period, the less risky stocks become.

Figure 5.2 S&P 500 Performance Over 50 Years

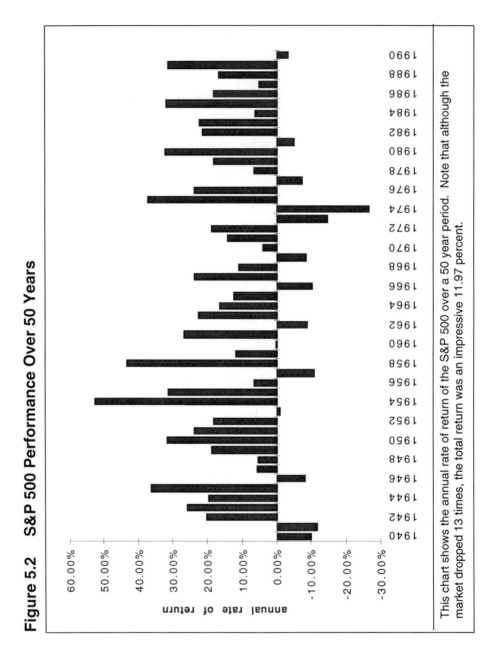

This chart shows the annual rate of return of the S&P 500 over a 50 year period. Note that although the market dropped 13 times, the total return was an impressive 11.97 percent.

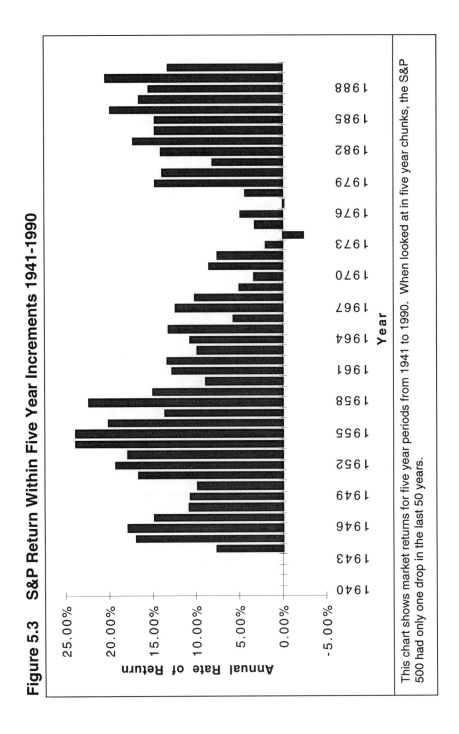

Figure 5.3   S&P Return Within Five Year Increments 1941-1990

This chart shows market returns for five year periods from 1941 to 1990. When looked at in five year chunks, the S&P 500 had only one drop in the last 50 years.

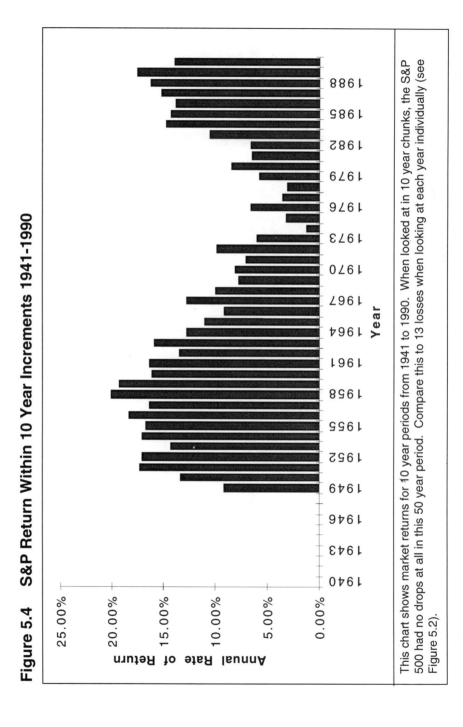

Figure 5.4   S&P Return Within 10 Year Increments 1941-1990

This chart shows market returns for 10 year periods from 1941 to 1990. When looked at in 10 year chunks, the S&P 500 had no drops at all in this 50 year period. Compare this to 13 losses when looking at each year individually (see Figure 5.2).

How To Build Wealth With Your 401(k)

Bond Returns

From our earlier discussion you know that bonds offer a fixed-interest rate but are subject to price fluctuations when interest rates change. Remember that when interest rates rise, the price of bonds drop. From Table 5.3 you know that corporate bonds have had a higher return than government bonds and that bonds in general have not always kept ahead of inflation. Figure 5.5 shows bond returns over the 50 year period from 1941 to 1990. Bonds have posted several periods of loss over this same period. These losses were not as steep as the losses seen by the stock market, but of course the gains were not as substantial either.

Long-term government bonds had 16 years of negative returns since 1941. The losses were generally very small and averaged -2.95 percent. The 50 year average annual return was 4.41 percent. Corporate bonds returned an annual 4.9 percent and experienced 14 years of negative annual returns. The average of all negative returns was -2.83 percent.

Historically, bonds have performed modestly over any period of time. This is the nature of the investment vehicle, but the 1980's were an exception. During this time, long-term bonds performed as well as or slightly better than stocks. This was the first time ever that bonds outperformed stocks over a long period of time. However, when you start expanding the period to 15, 20, 25 years or longer, bonds performed poorly in comparison.

The 1980's were a strange decade for bonds. Inflation was high in the late 1970's and early 1980's so bond owners were getting high returns. Prevailing market rates began to drop and bond owners were left with high interest bearing investments. In 1982 government bonds returned 40.3 percent. It's hard to tell what the future will bring. It is unlikely we will see a repeat of the 1980's. If rates start spiraling upward, bond funds will perform poorly.

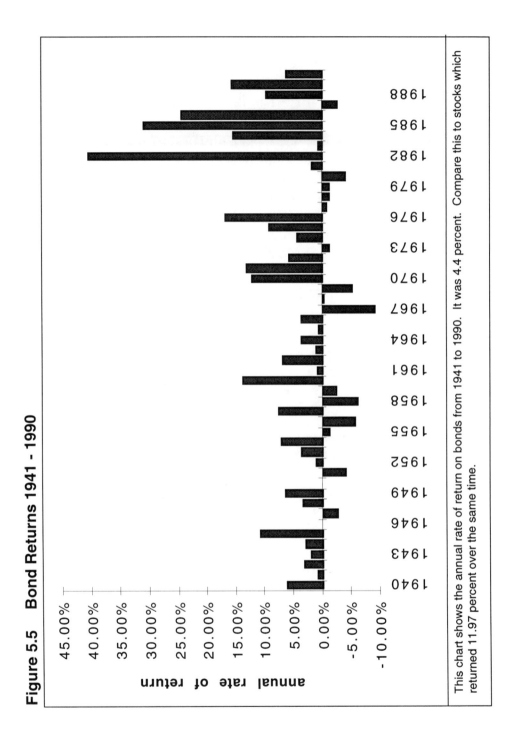

Figure 5.5   Bond Returns 1941 - 1990

This chart shows the annual rate of return on bonds from 1941 to 1990. It was 4.4 percent. Compare this to stocks which returned 11.97 percent over the same time.

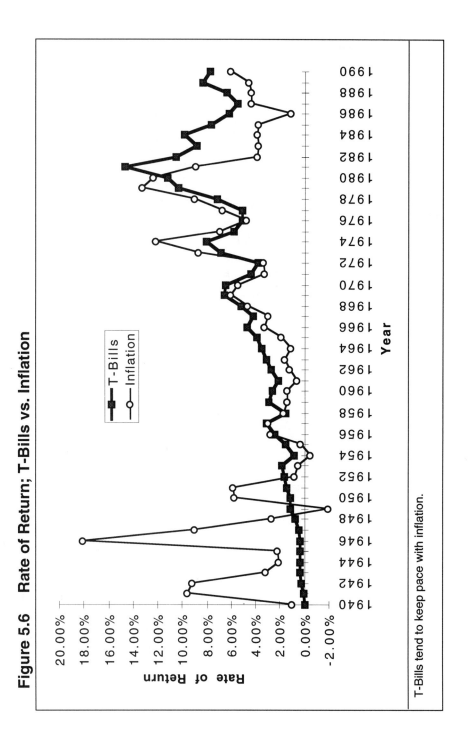

Figure 5.6   Rate of Return; T-Bills vs. Inflation

T-Bills tend to keep pace with inflation.

Most investors purchase bonds through bond funds. Bond funds actively trade bonds to take advantage of capital gains. This increases the potential for higher returns and, at the same time, increases risk.

Cash Equivalents

The most popular cash equivalent investment is the Treasury Bill. Treasury Bill rates change as market rates rise and fall. They are short-term investments that return a rate close to inflation. See Figure 5.6 for a comparison of Treasury Bills to inflation.

Chapter 6

401(k) Portfolio Management

If you own more than one type of an investment, then you have a portfolio. Your portfolio could contain real estate, mutual funds, retirement investments and any other investment vehicle. Managing all your investments is called **portfolio management**. It entails selecting investments to match your objectives, weeding out poor performers and monitoring the overall performance of your entire portfolio.

To get started, you need objectives. We talked about objectives in an earlier chapter, but let's take a look at some specific examples. A young, dual-income couple with no children can afford to invest aggressively for long-term capital appreciation. A couple with several growing children needs to invest for the future, but should have some money in low-risk, liquid investments in case of emergencies. Retired couples generally want current income and have low risk tolerances. You can see that your choice of investments should largely be determined by your life-style and your ambitions. No two households will have the same investment strategy.

Choosing the best mix of investments to meet your needs is very important. For example, if you plan to retire in 30 years and invest solely in bonds, you will probably end up very disappointed. On the other hand, a large bond holding may be suitable for a retiree living on a fixed income. If you have just retired you may need to mix a few stocks into your portfolio. This will help protect against inflation for the next 20 years or so. Look at Table 5.3 once again to see how bonds performed in comparison to other investments over a 60 year time frame.

Real-Life Asset Allocation

Selecting which investments to add to your holdings is called **asset allocation**. Asset allocation lets you build a portfolio that provides current income as well as capital appreciation. Asset allocation also limits how much you depend on any one type of investment. You can get both current income and capital appreciation by holding a combination of stocks and bonds to suit your needs. If you want more capital appreciation, then increase your holdings in growth stocks. If you want more current income, decrease your stock holdings or only buy stocks with large dividends.

If you spread your holdings over different investments, you don't need to worry as much about any one asset class performing poorly. If it does, you will most likely hold another asset that is doing well and can offset the loser. Table 6.1 shows the type of returns you can expect from different combinations of investments. Use it to help determine what mixture is best for you.

Different investment mixes produce different results as well as

Table 6.1   Asset Allocation Returns 1941-1990

Portfolio	Asset Mix	Number of Down Years	1941-1990 Average Loss in Down Year	Worst 1-Year Loss	Average Annual Return
Aggressive	100% Stocks	13	-9.61%	-26.27%	11.93%
Growth	75% Stocks / 25% Bonds	12	-7.11%	-18.76%	10.08%
Balanced	50% Stocks / 50% Bonds	11	-4.38%	-11.06%	8.19%
Income	25% Stocks / 75% Bonds	11	-2.19%	-5.53%	6.30%
Conservative	100% Bonds	16	-2.95%	-9.17%	4.41%

This table shows the type of returns you can expect from different combinations of investments. Notice that the greater your stock holding, the greater your return. Figures are based on Ibbotson and Associates data for the S&P 500 index and long-term government bonds different risk exposures. By adjusting the asset mix you can select trade-offs between short-term volatility and long-term returns. A portfolio invested 100 percent in stocks gives you the greatest potential for short-term volatility, but it also gives you the greatest opportunity for high returns. A portfolio containing all bonds offers the lowest short-term volatility, but you also reduce your opportunity for long-term gains. As you decrease the stocks you hold, you decrease short-term volatility but you also sacrifice the potential for long-term gains. This is the risk / return trade-off that all investors face.

There are no black and white answers to asset allocation and hindsight is always 20 / 20.

Many combinations of investments are used in asset allocation. If you ask 100 investment advisors for their favorite mix you will probably get 100 different responses. The answers may range from 100 percent stocks to 100 percent bonds. You may even be told to keep it all in cash and stash it neatly under your mattress. It's up to you to decide which mix is best for you.

Knowledge and experience offer the best way to determine your own personal asset allocation.

Selecting your asset allocation mix can be difficult. Your decision should take into account all your investments. It should also meet your long-, mid- and short-term investment goals. Remember to include savings accounts, money market accounts, certificate of deposits, savings bonds, brokerage accounts, IRA's and annuities along with your 401(k) plan. Your 401(k) money should be viewed as just one piece of the entire asset allocation model.

Your 401(k) is a vehicle to invest your long-term money. It is only one part of your total asset allocation plan.

The Early Years

If you have 10 or more years to retirement, then your 401(k) should be considered a long-term investment. Because you want your account to produce long-term growth, you should emphasize equities. It can even be argued to invest your account 100 percent in equities. The reasoning is that the further you are from retirement the less you should worry about short-term market fluctuations because you have the opportunity to achieve higher results in the long-term. The object is to maximize returns without trying to minimize short-term volatility.

Investing for short- and mid-term needs should be done outside your 401(k). It is important to have liquid short-term savings squirreled away, but not in your 401(k). Having 30 percent of your 401(k) assets invested in money markets for 10 to 40 years buys you nothing. You will probably get back the same real dollar value of the money that you put in. Nothing ventured, nothing gained!

It makes no sense for someone far from retirement to have 401(k) funds in a money market account. This investment will have low returns and probably return no gain in real dollar terms.

Pre-Retirement and Retirement

During retirement, most investors will probably want their 401(k) to provide current income and stability of principle. This requires a different asset allocation then investing for growth. As retirement nears, adjust your 401(k) investments to seek stability of principle. This allows you to transition from growth to current income. It also prevents you from having a large loss of principle due to short-term market fluctuations.

Money markets and stable funds make sense near retirement. You can still get tax deductions by contributing to your 401(k) while maintaining stability of principle by using a money market fund. Keep in mind that you may be in a lower tax bracket during retirement when you make withdrawals which gives you additional tax savings.

If you do not intend to use your 401(k) money as soon as you retire, then you should leave the funds invested in something other than a money market. It is important to maintain growth opportunities by investing in growth funds in order to keep pace with inflation. Even when retired, you will probably be investing for another 20 or 30 years. Long-term growth is still important. Keeping your money in the 401(k) or using an IRA rollover will allow you to maintain tax-deferred growth.

Market Timing vs. Systematic Investing

"Buy low, sell high" is the greatest investment advice ever given. If we could buy when the market is low and sell when it peaks, we'd be very wealthy. Unfortunately, it can't be done. Many have tried and many have failed.

Research shows that accounts using market timing do not provide better results than those using a buy and hold strategy. The "market timing" accounts actually perform worse when taking into account expenses. A study of the 1982 to 1987 bull market performed by the University of Michigan shows why market timing does not work. During this period, the five year bull market produced an average annual return of 26 percent as measured by the S&P 500 stock index.

If you were trying to time the market during this period and had your money pulled out during the 10 best days, your return would have dropped from 26 percent to 18 percent. If you missed the 40 best days your return would have dropped even further to 4 percent! When you consider that the 40 best days were spread out over the five year period and that the market moved quickly and unpredictably, you will see that it is nearly impossible to predict market performance. Only 40 days in a five year period accounted for a difference between a 26 percent annual return and a 4 percent annual return. You can't always be in the right place at the right time when you are constantly moving your money in and out of an unpredictable market.

Moving your money out of investments that are down as the result of a market correction only increases the probability you will miss large gains when the market comes back. Instead, why not take advantage of the market and buy more when the prices are low? A technique called **systematic investing** allows you to do just that.

Systematic investing has been used by successful investors for many years. The technique is simple. You continue contributing to your investments regardless of how the overall financial markets are doing. This method has become very popular and is also known as **dollar cost averaging**.

By dollar cost averaging you are buying less when the market is expensive and more when prices are low. This usually results in a lower price per share and increases your profits. By making contributions on a regular basis you are also reducing the influence of emotion that distorts your thinking when the market fluctuates. When you invest in a 401(k) you automatically have systematic investing working for you.

What You Need to Know About Mutual Funds

If you are like most investors, you probably won't build a portfolio of individual securities. Instead, you will likely invest in mutual funds. In a **mutual fund**, your money is pooled with other individual investors and a professional is hired to manage it. You get instant diversification with a small amount of money.

Today there are more than 7,000 retail mutual funds available to investors. A **retail fund** is one that is sold to the individual investor either directly or through a broker. There are many other institutional funds. An **institutional fund** is not typically sold to individual investors but instead is available through pension funds, 401(k) plans and profit sharing plans. When investing in a 401(k), you typically have a choice of several different mutual funds. Your company may offer retail funds, institutional funds, or a combination of both. There may also be a company stock fund to choose from.

You have many options to choose from when investing in mutual funds, but most funds generally fall into three general categories: equity, bond, and money market funds. The following sections describe the different categories of equity and bond funds typically found in 401(k) plans. Your 401(k) may offer more choices than what is listed.

Equity Funds

Equity funds consist of aggressive growth, growth, growth and income, index funds, balanced funds and foreign funds.

Aggressive growth funds seek maximum capital appreciation without concern for current income. They usually invest in fast growing companies and may use financial leverage techniques to increase returns. These funds are usually not very diversified so that they can take advantage of a fast growing segment of an industry. They invest in smaller stocks and may be called Capital Appreciation Funds. Aggressive growth funds assume very high risk in an effort to achieve very high returns. Their returns will typically be greater than the S&P 500 when the market is rising and lower when it's falling. They can be very volatile. An aggressive growth fund may have a beta of around 1.6 or more. Remember that beta is used to measure how volatile a stock is in relation to the market.

Growth funds seek long-term capital appreciation. They usually invest in stocks of growing companies that are established and have a strong market presence. Growth funds, unlike aggressive growth funds, typically do not use financial techniques and are more diversified. Growth funds try to outperform the S&P 500 and provide a higher total return over a long time frame. The beta in this type of fund may range from 0.9 to 1.2 and higher.

Growth and income funds try to provide long-term growth and current income while attempting to avoid large fluctuations of value. They generally invest in blue chip stocks, utilities, preferred stocks and convertible bonds. These funds are usually very diversified. *Equity income funds* have similar objectives but concentrate on dividend paying stocks. The beta for growth and income funds ranges between 0.8 and 1.1.

Index funds attempt to provide returns that correspond to a particular index. The most common index to mirror is the S&P 500. This type of index gives the optimal risk and return trade-offs. It is also referred to as an *index equity fund.* These types of funds are basically unmanaged funds. You buy the stocks in an index and do not try to outperform the market. Index funds usually have lower expenses because they are easy to manage. The S&P 500 index fund should have a beta of one.

Balanced funds have several objectives. They are concerned with preservation of principle while providing long-term growth of principle and current income. They generally invest in a mix of stocks and bonds. The mix may range from 50 / 50 to all stock or all bonds. A balanced fund is typically less volatile than an equity fund and it usually provides a better return than a bond fund.

Foreign funds come in different flavors. Funds called *foreign* or *international* buy securities outside of the United States. Global funds and worldwide funds buy foreign and United States securities.

Bond Funds

The objective of a bond fund is to provide current income through interest payments and, to a lesser extent, capital gains. Even if bond funds values decline due to market interest rate increases, current income is gained by the interest payments.

There are several types of bond funds. The most common are long-term, intermediate- and short-term funds. The type of bonds are commonly a mixture of government and investment grade corporate bonds. Bond fund returns fluctuate with interest rates.

Government bond funds are usually categorized as long-, intermediate-, or short-term. They provide current income and are considered to have no credit risk. The return on this type of fund will be slightly less than corporate bond funds with the same objective.

Corporate bond funds consist of investment grade corporate bonds with various maturities. The bond ratings should be "AA" or better for a high-grade fund. Investment grade bonds produce a slightly higher return than government bonds.

High-yield bond funds invest in lower rated investment grade or speculative grade corporate bonds. The fund achieves a higher return by assuming the higher risk associated with lower rated bonds. Bond ratings in high yield funds may range from single "A" to "BB" for conservative funds to "BB" or "CCC" for aggressive funds. High yield bond funds are volatile.

Fixed-income funds, also known as stable value funds, offer protection of principle and minimal price fluctuations. Fixed-income funds generally have different objectives. They are sometimes made up partly or completely of guaranteed investment contracts (GIC). Fixed-income funds try to maintain price stability. The return does not fluctuate over a short time frame. Fixed-income funds can also post returns that are a few percentage points above retail bond funds and money markets. This type of investment can be a good choice for individuals who are close to retiring or who have already done so. You will have a difficult time finding an investment broker or retail mutual fund that can beat the high return and lower risk associated with fixed and stable funds found in some 401(k) plans.

A **Guaranteed Investment Contract** (GIC) is an insurance company product issued for specific periods of time at fixed interest rates. The money is used to invest in other areas. The holder of a GIC is guaranteed a fixed rate of return as long as the insurance company stays solvent. Insurance companies are rated similar to bonds. A rating of "AA" or better indicates the insurance company is in good financial condition. Lower ratings show that the insurance company may (or is) having trouble meeting its obligations. Like lower rated bonds, you are at a higher risk and may lose your principle and remaining interest payments if the insurance company defaults. DO NOT BE MISLEAD BY THE WORD GUARANTEED.

If you are investing in a GIC, make sure the issuing insurance company is in good financial condition. It should be rated "AA" or better. Your portfolio should contain GICs from several different insurers in order to diversify away from unsystematic risk. The GIC offers a stable rate of return over a defined period.

Benchmarking and Mutual Funds

If you have a portfolio of stocks or bonds as an investment, how do you know how well they are performing? Is a 10 percent return good? How about a 30 percent return? A 30 percent gain is great as long as similar investments don't have a 50 percent gain! What about losses? Is a 10 percent loss bad? The answer is maybe yes or maybe no! It all depends on how your fund performed compared to the standard for that type of fund, as well as how the financial market for that type of investment performed.

From the previous chapter, you know that the performance of individual stocks and bonds can be evaluated using benchmarking. Mutual funds can be evaluated the same way. Benchmarking will help you better understand the differences between your 401(k) funds so that you can be more comfortable with your selection choices.

As a past performance indicator, benchmarking will show which of your funds have been able to meet or exceed their category averages in the past. By looking at historical results you can get an idea of how funds with different objectives provide different returns. Past performance is not used to predict the future and there is no guarantee that a fund will meet its stated objective. You cannot control the actual returns produced by the markets so there is no sense in trying to predict them. Past performance can however, be used to determine whether or not a fund has been able to meet its objective as compared to both the market and to category returns.

A fund that has lagged it's category average for a five- or ten-year period is probably going to continue to under-perform. It can be very damaging to select a fund with an objective of beating the S&P 500 Index only to find that it never reaches its goal. If your fund is lagging behind its category average over a five year period, then you are getting less return for your level of risk. In other words, you are losing the opportunity to receive better gains in another fund or category.

To measure performance of a fund you need at least a three- to five-year history. A new fund may come out and have a good performance for one year then spend the next four years in the cellar. Likewise, a fund may have one poor year, yet produce an excellent three- to five-year performance record. The reason that three to five years is used is that it suggests how well the fund's management can perform in different market conditions. Different investment styles and types of stocks go in and out of favor over time. Plus, the market is very dynamic. The longer a fund has been around, the easier it is to evaluate how well it is managed.

Once again, the past rate of return for a fund is no guarantee of future returns. We invest in equities because we believe they will continue to out perform other types of investments. The reason to look at past performance is to evaluate how likely a given fund will meet it's objective. If the market rises 20 percent and our fund increases 25 percent that's great. If the market drops 10 percent and our fund falls 12 percent that's OK. But if the market has risen 10 percent per year over the past five years and our fund has only returned 4 percent per year then there's a problem. The problem is not with the market returns, but with the fund itself. This is what we want to avoid when investing in mutual funds. And this is what we are trying to evaluate by looking at a funds past performance and comparing it to the benchmarks.

Each category of mutual funds has an average performance measurement calculated for it and its called a **category average**. Mutual funds are generally expected to perform in relation to their respective category averages and in accordance with the corresponding broad-based market index. Table 6.2 shows performance ratings for the last five year returns plus the 3, 5, and 10 year average annual returns. Use this table to examine how each category of equity funds has performed in comparison to the S&P 500 index. The foreign index shown in the table is the Morgan Stanley World Index. The Lehman

Table 6.2   Mutual Fund Performance Ratings

Fund Category	1995	1994	1993	1992	1991	1990	3 YR	5 YR	10 YR
Equity Funds									
Aggressive Growth	33.49	-3.31	18.02	8.76	50.42	-8.0	15.06	20.04	13.95
Growth	30.83	-2.04	11.54	8.36	36.74	-5.09	12.65	16.20	13.22
Growth & Income	31.60	-1.33	10.89	8.27	28.78	-4.68	12.92	14.96	12.33
Equity-Income	29.45	-1.98	13.41	9.39	27.23	-6.25	12.90	14.90	11.83
Asset Allocation	23.91	-3.14	15.58	6.13	20.84	-0.83	11.53	12.21	11.39
Balanced	24.80	-2.81	13.40	7.05	26.44	-0.58	11.21	13.24	11.43
World Stock	15.81	-2.92	31.63	-0.68	18.4	-10.83	13.96	11.72	11.65
Market Indexes									
MSCI World	20.72	5.08	22.50	-5.22	18.28	-17.12	15.83	11.74	13.09
S&P 500	37.53	1.31	10.06	7.7	30.33	-3.11	15.32	16.57	14.84
LB Bond Aggregate	18.47	-2.92	9.75	7.24	16	8.94	8.07	9.44	9.61

Use this chart to compare the performance of your mutual funds. The MSCI World index is a world market equity fund indicator. The S&P 500 is your equity fund benchmark. Use the LB (Lehman Brothers) Bond Aggregate index to weed out equity funds that are poor performers. Remember that a good equity fund will outperform the bond index. All returns are total returns for the period ending Dec 31. Source: Fund Category Annual Return Data from Morningstar, Inc.; Indexes from respective Companies

Brothers Bond Aggregate index is used for bond fund comparison.

Table 6.2 shows that you should expect equities as a whole to outperform bonds. You should also expect aggressive growth and growth funds to outperform the S&P 500 over time. Look at the big difference in performance between the S&P 500 and the aggressive growth category. When the stock market is rising, the aggressive growth category rises much faster (compare 1991, and 1993). Now look at 1990. When the market is falling the aggressive growth fund falls much faster (-8 percent vs. -3.11 percent for the S&P 500).

You can see that there is more fluctuation in the aggressive growth category, but there is also the opportunity for bigger returns. Now look at the five-year average annual rate of return of the S&P 500 compared to the aggressive growth category. The S&P 500 returned 16.57 percent while the average aggressive growth fund returned 20.04 percent. If you were in an aggressive growth fund that performed at its category average or better, then you would have achieved substantial gains over this period of time.

In exchange for the higher return expected from growth and aggressive growth funds, you are taking on the risk that an actively managed fund will outperform the market over time. The market is measured by the S&P 500 which is conceptually an unmanaged fund. An index fund that tracks the S&P 500 can be considered to represent the optimum risk vs. return for stock funds. This type of fund has a beta of one which means it follows the market as it goes up and down.

Category averages indicate how well a fund is performing in relation to other funds of the same type. Within each category there will be a wide spread of returns even though the funds have the same stated objectives. Each category is typically composed of top, average, and poor performers. It is very important to be able to pick the top performers so that you can optimize the amount of return you receive in exchange for the risk you assume. For example, if your aggressive growth fund is a poor performer, you could probably find a balanced or index equity fund returning the same rate but with less risk. In other words, if you are assuming the higher risk associated with an aggressive growth fund, then you should expect a higher return. If you are not getting that higher return over a three- to five-year period, then you are better off in another fund category that offers less risk for the same or even better return.

Let's move to another table. Table 6.3 shows how differently funds within the same category can perform. All the funds in this table are growth funds. Funds are listed in order from the best performers at the top to the poorest performers at the bottom. The funds listed are real funds and these are their actual performance numbers, but the names were left out to protect the innocent!

When looking at Table 6.3, use the S&P 500 index as your reference for the overall stock market. The Lehman Brothers Aggregate, which is a bond market benchmark, is also included in the table for your reference. If you compare the poorly performing growth funds to the bond index returns you will see that they didn't produce a significantly better return than the bond funds. This is distressing when you consider that equities, especially growth equities, historically out perform bonds. Not only that, the last 10 years has been very good for equities. It sure doesn't make sense to assume the higher risk associated with a growth fund when you can get similar results with less risk in a bond fund. In other words, stay away from the losers.

As explained earlier, past performance allows you to evaluate how a fund performed in comparison to similar funds. Only about 20 percent of the available funds have outperformed the S&P 500 index. You may want to avoid any fund that has severely lagged its own category average over a long time. Although a fund that has performed poorly the last ten years could certainly turn around and be the top performer for the next ten years, it is highly unlikely. If a fund is unable to beat the S&P 500 over time, then it might be a good idea to invest in the S&P 500 index fund.

Remember, you can beat 80 percent of professional fund managers by investing in an S&P 500 index fund.

Table 6.3   Performance Deviation Between Funds In the Same Category

Fund Category	1995	1994	1993	1992	1991	1990	3 YR	5 YR	10 YR
Equity Funds									
Fund A	36.28	-1.12	21.43	15.89	54.92	3.94	17.84	24.05	19.38
Fund B	36.82	-1.81	24.66	7.02	41.03	-4.51	18.75	20.38	17.42
Fund C	29.43	-1.1	10.88	6.87	42.8	-0.74	12.38	16.72	15.57
Fund D	28.71	1.47	11.32	6.3	36.05	-7.57	13.29	16.02	12.74
Fund E	27.34	-2.97	12.29	5.21	30.76	-3.76	11.53	13.8	11.71
Fund F	32.94	-1.35	8.5	3.68	26.73	-8.96	12.48	13.33	11.44
Fund G	28.21	1.05	-0.52	3.74	67.54	N/A	8.33	17.5	N/A
Market Indexes									
S&P 500	37.53	1.31	10.06	7.7	30.33	-3.11	15.32	16.57	14.84
LB Bond Aggregate	18.47	-2.92	9.75	7.24	16	8.94	8.07	9.44	9.61

This chart shows that funds within the same investment category can have very different results. The Growth Fund Index is an average of all the individual growth funds. You can see that some funds perform better than the index, and some perform worse. Some of these growth funds actually performed worse than the LB (Lehman Brothers) Aggregate which is a bond market index. Growth funds are listed in order from best to worst performers. All returns are total returns for the period ending Dec 31.

Long-Term Performance

Do not be concerned with short-term fluctuations in your funds. Keep your sights on long-term growth so you can achieve higher rates of returns. It is helpful to look at what is known as *average annual rates of return* which provides an average annual rate of return over a given period of time. This type of averaging takes into account single year fluctuations over several years. Table 6.2 shows 3, 5, and 10 year average annual rates of return.

Individual annual rates of return for the S&P 500 index over the five-year period from 1991 to 1995 were 30.33 percent, -7.7 percent, 10.06 percent, 1.31 percent and 37.53 percent. You can see that these returns cover a very wide range. The average annual return for this five-year period is 16.57 percent which is calculated by using a formula called the **geometric means**. You will learn how to calculate this formula in the next chapter.

The average annual rate of return shows that earning the drastically different annual rates of return over the five years from 1991 to 1995 is essentially the same as earning a constant 16.57 percent for each of those years *if you stayed invested for the full five years!* If you look at it as a five year investment returning 16.57 percent, that one year return of 1.31 percent doesn't seem so bad! Not only that, but if you removed your money from the market after the 1.31 percent return, you would have missed the 37.53 percent return achieved the following year! The average annual rate of return for a specified period allows you to smooth out individual yearly returns and look at the returns over a longer period.

401(k) Investment Options

Most 401(k) plans have three basic investment options to choose from. Some have an additional company stock fund. Other options are often added on to the basic three. Your company may have as many as eight or more choices. The three basic investment options are *diversified equity fund, fixed-income fund,* and *money market fund.* The company stock fund invests exclusively in the stock of the company you are working for.

The **diversified equity fund** most often found in 401(k) plans is usually an index fund that tracks the S&P 500 or a growth fund. The fund may be referred to as a diversified equity fund, an equity fund, or an index equity fund. You can identify this type of fund by reading the investment objectives provided by your company.

The **fixed income fund** usually invests in short to intermediate government bonds and GICs. Many of the bond funds tend to be weighted in U.S. Treasury issues. Interest rate returns in a fixed fund are more stable. The investment account value does not vary much. If you are investing in fixed-income funds containing GICs be sure to look at the quality of the insurance company that issued the investment. It should be rated AA or higher. A fixed income fund should contain several different GICs so that credit risk can be reduced by diversification.

Money market funds invest in various cash equivalents or short-term government securities. This type of fund offers stability in investment value and typically has a rate of return close to the T-Bill rate.

In addition to the basic three investment options, your company may add a **growth fund** to the 401(k) plan. This option improves your opportunity to achieve greater returns than what is typically offered by an index equity fund. A **foreign equity fund** may also be included to allow investing in markets outside the United States. Foreign funds provide even greater diversification to your portfolio. They also have the additional systematic risk associated with fluctuating currency values. Tables 6.4 and 6.5 show two sample 401(k) plan options. The first example has three options. The second has seven. Funds are listed from the greatest risk and return first to the least risk and return last.

As 401(k) plans continue to grow rapidly in popularity, you will likely find your company adding more investment choices. Be sure to evaluate your fund choices and build an investment strategy that will accomplish your financial objectives. You will learn more about this in the next chapter.

Keep in mind that there are no guarantees that a fund will meet it's stated objective. Actual performance of one fund may be poor in relation to other funds of the same type. As discussed in the last chapter, benchmarking is a very good way to measure the performance of your investments. Let's take a look at this investment tool in relation to your 401(k).

Table 6.4   Basic 401(k) Options

Fund	Objective
Index Equity Fund	Match the S&P 500
Fixed-income Fund	Invest in Guaranteed Investment Contracts or short-term government bills or notes.
Money Market Fund	Invest in cash equivalents

Table 6.5   401(k) With More Options

Fund	Objective
Foreign Stock	Invest in equities in foreign companies
Growth Fund	Beat the S&P 500
Index Equity Fund	Match the S&P 500
Balanced Fund	Invest in a mix of stocks and bonds
Intermediate Bond	Invest in bonds of intermediate length
Fixed-income Fund	Invest in Guaranteed Investment Contracts
Money Market Fund	Invest in cash equivalents

Can a Managed Fund Beat the S&P 500?

The subject of whether or not a managed fund can consistently beat the market as represented by the S&P 500 over a long period of time is fiercly debated. Many believe that it can not be done. The fact that only about 20 percent of actively managed funds do better than the market as measured by the S&P 500 adds to the debate. Different categories may beat the S&P 500 in any given year or possibly for a three- or five-year period, but as you start looking at longer periods, the S&P 500 performs just as well or even better than managed funds. Look at the 3, 5, and 10 year performance history in Table 6.2

There are several reasons for this. First the S&P 500 is made up of a broad spectrum of different types of stocks. It will consistently perform as an average of the individual types and classifications of the stocks that it is made of. Funds that try to outperform the market are looking for the faster growing stocks in different industries and sectors. Although the selected stocks may have much better one- or three-year performances it is difficult to always be in the right place at the right time. It also costs money. Trading is expensive. This is reflected by high management fees which drag down the fund's performance. There are some funds that have beaten the market over a period of ten years or more but they are the exception not the rule. Whether or not a managed fund can continue to beat the market over a long period of time is yet to be determined.

With this in mind, an S&P 500 index fund is an excellent fund to build your investment foundation upon. It provides an optimum risk / return trade-off and you will not have to worry about how well your fund manager is performing.

If your 401(k) has a top performing growth or aggressive growth fund to choose from, than this is another good option for your 401(k) portfolio. You will assume a higher risk but you also get the potential for higher returns. You have already seen what a 3 or 4 percent higher rate of return will mean to your final account value. To jog your memory, if you put $1,000 into an investment and let it grow for 30 years at a rate of 8 percent, your final account value will be $10,062. If the same investment returns 12 percent, your final account value will be $29,959! The opportunity to assume a higher risk in exchange for a potentially higher return is necessary if you intend to accumulate great wealth.

Other Criteria Used to Select Investments

So far our discussion on 401(k) investment selection has been limited to historical performance and risk categorization. There are other elements used to evaluate investment selection such as fund expenses, management, quantitative risk measurement and tax distribution. Performance and risk, in my opinion, are clearly the most significant elements in 401(k) investment selection because they take into account all the other elements. By looking at past performance you can get a feel for how well the fund has been managed in the past.

The other elements used to evaluate investment selection (expenses, management, and tax distribution) do not need to be discussed at length because you have no control over them when investing in your 401(k). You are also limited to the investment selections available. In a 401(k) you do not have a full range of substitute funds to choose from. Once again, the best way to evaluate a 401(k) fund's ability to meet its objectives is to look at its past performance. Of course this does not guarantee that it will perform well in the future, but it certainly increases the probability.

I look at it this way. Suppose you are about to have major surgery performed. Would you rather go to the hospital that has been performing the surgery successfully for the past ten years or to the new hospital that is new to the operation? Certainly both can succeed and both could fail, but it is nice to know the one you are going to has been successful in the past.

An organization, such as a hospital or a mutual fund, is successful for many different reasons. The managers, staff, procedures, and philosophies all contribute to its success. An organization that remains successful over a long period of time is one that has been able to make adjustments to its operations as needed. Every element within an organization contributes to its success. This is true of hospitals, baseball teams, and mutual funds.

One more point in our hospital analogy. If you had a hospital whose success rate was less than the average for its type of operation and one that was above average which would you prefer to go to? Enough said!

For those of you who think you cannot compare hospitals and investments, you have obviously never felt the pain of losing money!

How To Build Wealth With Your 401(k)

Chapter 7

Create Your Own Plan

Now it's time to tie together everything you have learned about 401(k) investing in order to select funds from within your own plan. At this point you have all the knowledge and analytical tools you need to make informed investment decisions. Congratulations! In this chapter you will learn how to prepare your own 401(k) analysis.

Let's recap everything you've learned so far. For starters, you know how your particular plan works with regards to plan mechanics, i.e. eligibility, vesting schedules, contribution rates, loans and withdrawals. You know that the 401(k) has several powerful advantages, such as tax breaks, employer match, and convenience. In an earlier chapter, you filled out a worksheet identifying how much you can contribute to your account, how much additional money you get in the form of a company match, and what the dollar amount of your tax savings is.

Next, you learned investment fundamentals such as how to set investment objectives, the time value of money, compound interest, inflation, taxes, the risk / return trade-off, and diversification. You acquired several useful analytical tools that allow you to measure investment performance. Examples include present value, future value, and benchmarking. At this point, you know that stocks, bonds, and cash equivalents are the three basic types of investments. You know that these three types of investments all perform differently and are used to meet different investment objectives.

More recently, you learned basic portfolio management techniques, such as asset allocation, systematic investing, and mutual fund investing. You even know how to categorize mutual funds by investment objectives. With all this knowledge under your belt, you should feel very confident about your ability to make good investment decisions. So, let's put this information to use by making a real-life plan for *your* 401(k) investments!

The overall objective is to select the types of funds that best suits your needs and to select the best funds available. In the real world, these two objectives may not coincide. For example, you may want an aggressive growth fund but the only one that's available may be a poor performer. Luckily, in my history of researching and evaluating 401(k) investment funds, I have never come across a plan with only poor funds to choose from. Most plans offer at least an index equity type fund that tracks the S&P 500. The investment options I have seen range from excellent performers in their category, to the worst funds on the planet. Try to avoid the bad funds at all cost.

NOTE: If you are in a 403(b) or 401(k) plan containing a variable annuity contract please read the special section in Appendix C.

Organize Your Analysis on Paper

I have developed two worksheets to help you organize your entire 401(k) analysis. They can be found in Table 7.1 and Table 7.2. The first worksheet is for analyzing your equity funds. Along the left hand column is a list of each general category of equity funds, i.e. Aggressive Growth, Growth, Equity Income, and Growth & Income. The corresponding category fund averages over the past few years are already filled in for you. Your job is to determine which category each of your equity funds belong to and pencil them into the table. The next step is to fill in the corresponding performance history for each of your funds in the space provided.

Along the bottom of the worksheet found in Table 7.1 I have supplied you with performance data for the three relevant market indexes: S&P 500, Morgan Stanley Company World Index, and the NASDAQ Composite. As you know from earlier sections, the S&P 500 index tracks U.S. equities as a whole, the Morgan Stanley World Index is used to benchmark international funds, and the NASDAQ Composite is a small stock benchmark. Table 7.2 has the Lehman Brother's aggregate bond benchmark. Use it to weed out poorly performing equity funds (i.e. equity funds should outperform the bond index). You will notice that the worksheet does not contain category averages for foreign funds. This is because foreign funds are a very diverse group and cannot easily be lumped into an average rating.

Performance data already included in the worksheet is based on an ending period of Dec 31. Make sure that the annual rates of return for your company's funds is based on the same ending period. This is the most common ending period used at most companies. If your company uses an ending period other than December 31, you will need to create matching benchmark performance data. This can be done with data collected from the reference section of your local library. You may also want to refer to the section at the end of this chapter on where to go for help.

If you have already filled out the worksheets earlier in this book (Table 2.2) then all the information you need to fill out the analysis is at your fingertips. If not, take the time to collect the information. Everything you need should be available from your Human Resources department. Be sure to collect annual performance data for as far back as you can. Also be sure that performance data is based on year ending Dec 31, otherwise you will not be able to make comparisons using data provided in the worksheets.

Along the right hand side of the equity worksheet in Table 7.1 you will see columns for 3, 5, 8, and 10 year average rates of return. Again, some of the data has been supplied for you, but you will need to calculate returns for your own funds. The next few sections will show you how.

You may have some funds that have not been around for more than a year or two. If this is the case, then fill in as much of the worksheet as you can. Remember that it is not usually a good idea to invest in new funds because you have no idea how well they have performed in the past. Let someone else try them out before you do.

Table 7.1

Equity Fund Worksheet

Fund Category	1995	1994	1993	1992	1991	1990	1989	1988	1987	1986	3 YR	5 YR	8 YR	10 YR
Aggressive Growth	33.49	-3.31	18.02	8.76	50.42	-8	26.96	16.07	-3.16	12.79	15.06	20.04	16.44	13.95
Growth	30.83	-2.04	11.54	8.36	36.74	-5.09	26.81	114.85	2.64	15.21	12.65	16.2	14.37	13.22
Equity-Income	29.45	-1.98	13.41	9.39	27.23	-6.25	21.14	17.37	-2.12	17.11	12.9	14.9	10.82	11.83
Growth & Income	31.6	-1.33	10.89	8.27	28.78	-4.68	23.35	14.87	2.18	15.44	12.92	14.96	13.28	12.33
Market Indexes														
S&P 500	37.53	1.31	10.06	7.7	30.33	-3.11	31.59	16.5	5.18	18.62	15.32	16.57	15.64	14.84
NASDAQ Composite	39.92	-3.2	14.75	15.45	56.84	-17.8	19.26	15.41	-5.26	7.36	17.1	23.79	16.05	12.84
MSCI World	20.72	5.08	22.5	-5.22	18.28	-17.12	16.6	23.29	16.17	41.89	15.83	11.74	9.56	13.09

All returns are total returns for the period ending Dec 31. Use this worksheet to compare the investments in your 401(k). Source: Fund Category Annual Return Data from Morningstar, Inc.; Bond index from Lehman Brothers.

How To Build Wealth With Your 401(k)

Table 7.2   Hybrid and Bond Fund Worksheet

Fund Category	1995	1994	1993	1992	1991	1990	1989	1988	1987	1986	3 YR	5 YR	8 YR	10 YR
Asset Allocation	23.91	-3.14	15.58	6.13	20.84	-0.83	16.57	8.03	9.22	21.26	11.53	12.21	10.49	11.39
Balanced	24.8	-2.81	13.4	7.05	26.44	-0.58	19.59	12.22	1.78	16.76	11.21	13.24	12.05	11.43
Market Indexes														
S&P 500	37.53	1.31	10.06	7.7	30.33	-3.11	31.59	16.5	5.18	18.62	15.32	16.57	15.64	14.84
LB Bond Aggregate	18.47	-2.92	9.75	7.24	16	8.94	14.59	7.87	2.76	15.25	8.07	9.44	9.81	9.61
T-Bills	5.51	4.27	3.02	3.46	5.41	7.51	8.11	6.67	5.47	6.16	4.26	4.33	5.48	5.55

All returns are total returns for the period ending Dec 31. Source: Fund Category Annual Return Data from Morningstar, Inc.; Bond index from Lehman Brothers.

The second worksheet found in Table 7.2 is used to analyze your bond funds. It is very similar to the equities worksheet. Performance data for market indexes and category averages have already been filled in for you. You will notice that the balanced fund category is included in this worksheet. Because a balanced fund contains both stocks and bonds, this category could have been placed just as easily in the equity worksheet. A balanced fund is considered lower risk than a pure equity fund and a higher risk than a pure bond fund. Your job is to fill in data on the bond funds available in your company's 401(k) plan.

Now the Real Fun Begins!

After you have filled out the worksheets in Table 7.1 and Table 7.2 the real fun begins! All the data is at your fingertips and you have only to compare your funds against the corresponding benchmarks and category indexes. This will tell you if your funds are good, bad or average. Make sure you assign a red flag to any funds that lag the indexes, as well as any funds that are new. Also be wary of a new fund with a great one-year performance. Many funds start out with a good one-year performance than drop into the cellar for years to come.

When calculating a three- or five-year average annual return, if one year shows a much higher performance than the other years, your result will be misleading. Be sure to look closely at each yearly return. Two funds may have the same average annual return over a 3, 5, and 10-year period, but if one shows larger gains and losses over individual years, it is a much more volatile fund. You are assuming a higher risk than average for the return.

It's a very good idea to continue tracking your funds each year. Use the worksheets as templates and update benchmarks, category averages and fund performances each year. Ask your benefits office to provide the most current data for benchmarks or use the reference section at your public library to obtain the standard benchmarks and category averages. Or refer to the last section in this chapter on where to go for help.

There is a lot of gray area when defining what the objective of a fund is and placing it in a category. Each fund within a category has its own unique style of investing. Some funds may do better than others one year, then lag the pack the next. This could be because the investment manager's style is out of favor for a year or two or because the manager is positioning for future growth.

Do not panic if your fund is off its benchmark for a one-year period. Portfolio managers are continually adjusting their positions. If a fund has performed well in the past and is off one year, give the fund manager the benefit of the doubt. A five-year or greater average is a better measurement tool. On the other hand, if the market is rising year after year and your fund is still a loser, let someone else give the manager the benefit of the doubt. Move your money elsewhere.

Here is one final note with regard to evaluating 401(k) fund options. You should only be concerned with total return which includes dividends, interest, and capital gains. Mutual fund performance is reported this way which makes your job a little easier. Investment gains are taxed as ordinary income when distributed from a 401(k). It does not matter if the gains are from current income or capital gains.

How to Calculate the Average Annual Rate of Return

You will need to calculate the average annual rates of return when filling out the 3, 5, 8 and 10 year columns in the worksheets in Table 7.1 and Table 7.2. For example, when calculating the three-year average rate of return for one of your funds start by identifying what the annual return was for each of the three years. Your next inclination may be to add up the returns from those three years and divide by three ... don't do this! This method of calculation is an arithmetic average. It does not take into account compound interest and the results will be very wrong. You need to calculate the **geometric mean** which gives you the average annual rate of return over a span of years when the individual return for each year is different.

In just a minute I'll show you how the formula works and take you through a few examples. If you still find the math too frustrating to mess with, refer to the section at the end of this chapter on where to go for help.

Let's say you're evaluating a fund that returned 90 percent, -25 percent and 10 percent over the last three years. If you had invested money in this fund what would your average annual rate of return be at the end of the three-year period? Once again, ignore your first impulse to sum the numbers and divide by three. Let's work through the example using the geometric mean. The annual returns given are for the years ending 1994, 1995 and 1996.

Example 1

Year	Return
1994	90%
1995	-25%
1996	10%

Step 1 Express each of the three returns as a decimal.

0.90, -0.25, 0.10.

Step 2 Add 1.0 to each decimal value.

1.9, 0.75, 1.1

Step 3 Multiply the values in Step 2 together.

(1.9 x 0.75 x 1.1) = 1.568

Step 4a Calculate one divided by the number of years.

1 / 3 = 0.3333

Step 4b Calculate the result of y^x where y is the result of Step 3 and x is the result of Step 4a. Use the function y^x power on your calculator.

$1.568^{0.3333} = 1.1618$

Step 5 Subtract 1.0 from the result in Step 4.

1.1618 - 1 = 0.1618

Step 6 Multiply the result from Step 5 by 100 to express as a percentage.

0.1618 x 100 = 16.18%.

The final answer is 16.18 percent. It means that if you were in a fund that had three individual annual returns of 90 percent, - 25 percent and 10 percent it would be the same results as a fund that had a 16.18 percent return each year for the three-year period.

As I mentioned earlier, it would be incorrect to solve this problem using an arithmetic average, although this is a calculation you are probably more familiar with. Let's see what result the arithmetic average produces by summing up the three individual returns and dividing by the total number of years which in this example is three.

$$(0.90 + (-0.25) + 0.10) / 3 = 25\%.$$

This result of 25 percent is way off from our earlier calculation of 16.18 percent! Why? The reason is compound interest. The geometric mean takes into account the principle of compound interest, the arithmetic mean does not. Remember that your money is compounding as it sits in an investment over a multi-year period. The arithmetic mean can be very misleading if used to calculated average annual returns. The greater the spread of the individual numbers the greater the difference between the two methods of calculation.

Example 2

Let's calculate the three-year average annual rate of return for the S&P 500 index. Table 7.1 contains the individual annual rate of returns for the three year period from 1991 to 1993. They are:

Year	Return
1991	30.33%
1992	7.7%
1993	10.06%

Step 1 Express each of the returns as a decimal.

0.3033, 0.077, 0.1006

Step 2 Add 1.0 to each decimal value.

1.3033, 1.077. 1.1006

Step 3 Multiply the results from Step 2 together.

$$1.3033 \times 1.077 \times 1.1006 = 1.5448$$

Step 4a   Calculate one divided by the number of years.

$$1 / 3 = 0.3333$$

Step 4b   Calculate y^x where y is the result of Step 3 and x is the results of Step 4a.

$$1.5448^{0.3333} = 1.156$$

Step 5 Subtract one from the result of Step 4b.

$$1.156 - 1 = 0.156$$

Step 6 Multiply the result of Step 5 by 100 to express as a percentage.

$$0.1548 \times 100 = 15.6\%$$

The S&P 500 3 year average annual rate of return for the period ending December 31, 1993 was 15.6 percent.

Example 3

Now let's calculate the five-year average annual rate of return for the S&P 500 index. Again, the returns can be found in Table 7.1. They are:

Year	Return
1989	31.59%
1990	-3.11%
1991	30.33%
1992	7.7%
1993	10.06%

Step 1 0.3159, -0.0311, 0.3033, 0.077, 0.1006

Step 2 1.3159, 0.9689, 1.3033, 1.077, 1.1006

Step 3 $1.3159 \times 0.9689 \times 1.3033 \times 1.077 \times 1.1006 = 1.9697$

Step 4a $1 / 5 = 0.2000$

Step 4b $1.9697^{0.2000} = 1.1452$

Step 5 1.1452 - 1 = 0.1452

Step 6 0.1452 x 100 = 14.52%

The S&P 500 five-year average annual rate of return for the period ending Dec 31, 1993 was 14.52 percent.

You should now be able to calculate the average annual return for any period you have an interest in. This is a very useful tool. It allows you to evaluate the past performance of any fund. All you need is the historical annual rates of return associated with that fund and you can compare it to the past performance of any other funds in its category. Just make sure to use the same number of years and the same ending period when comparing two funds or when comparing a fund to an index. Also keep in mind that you cannot use an annual rate of return if the number does not represent performance over the entire year. You might run into this with new funds started in the middle of the year. You can use Table 7.1 to practice calculating average annual returns. Calculate the three- and five-year returns for the S&P 500 index for the period ending Dec 31, 1995 and refer to Table 7.1 for the answers.

Allocate Money Among Your 401(k) Funds

All right! Now you're ready to make the ultimate decision: how to allocate money among your 401(k) investment options. If you have completed the worksheets in Table 7.1 and Table 7.2, then you know what the objective of each of your funds is and how past performance compares to category averages and market benchmarks. In other words, you know what to expect from your funds and you know which are the winners and which are the losers. This information is critical. By making asset allocation decisions based on sound financial analysis, you can build a final account value with exciting proportions. Just think how much you're going to enjoy the money when you retire!

The first step is to determine your investment objective. If you are far from retirement, then you should be concerned with long-term growth. As you near time to begin account withdrawals, you should begin to transition into current income investments. Your first choice should be to select funds that match your objective, but if these funds are poor performers you should avoid them. For example, if you want to employ an aggressive growth strategy and the fund that matches this profile is a loser, then avoid it. You would be better off in an S&P 500 index fund. If you can't beat it, join it.

If you have more than one equity fund available, choose the best ones and diversify among them. An index equity fund tracking the S&P 500 is an excellent place to develop a foundation in equities. In your case, it may be the only equity fund available. This is fine as long as the fund really is tracking the S&P 500.

If you have more than one good equity fund to choose from, the S&P 500 index fund still makes sense as your equity foundation. From here you should diversify the rest of your equity money to other funds that seem to be good performers. This reduces the risk of having all your money in a fund that under performs its own category and under performs the market. Diversifying also increases your opportunity to achieve higher gains in more aggressive equity funds. Depending on your investment objective, you may want to appropriate more money toward a certain equity fund category.

By spreading contributions across several funds you decrease the risk of being in a fund that under performs the market due to management style or lack of ability to beat the market. Don't worry if a fund is off its mark for one year. The fund's investment style may be out of favor. Give the fund time to meet its long-term objectives. Remember, when you invest in equities you are looking for long-term gains. Do not panic at short-term fluctuations.

A word of caution. Don't try to chase a hot performing fund. Different management styles will do better than others in any given year (this is what is meant by *in favor* and *out of favor*). Make your selection, then hang in there. As long as your funds are good performers within their category, and the financial markets grow over time, your account will also grow. Individual investors who have built great wealth in the stock market are those disciplined enough to stay in when things look bad.

From time-to-time you may come into contact with a new fund. Perhaps the fund has been around for years but was just recently added to your plan. It may even be a brand new fund that was recently added to your options. If 401(k) benefits are new to your company all the funds will be new to you in one way or another. Similarly, you may have a new employer whose 401(k) options are all new to you. Be sure to evaluate each new investment as it presents itself. Request historical performance data as far back as possible. Add the new fund to your Performance Analysis Worksheets in Table 7.1 and Table 7.2 and base your allocation decision on the fund's value to your portfolio.

If a fund is newly formed, or has a history of less than three years, it is advisable to delay investing in it. There is no way of knowing whether or not the fund will meet its objectives. It could be very damaging to invest in a newly formed fund that turns out to be the worst performer in its category. If you leave your money in the new fund for three to five years and find out it's a loser, you end up losing the opportunity for growth that you could have had if you had invested in an S&P 500 index fund.

Real-Life 401(k) Asset Allocation Decisions

Let's look at a few examples of how 401(k) savings can be allocated among available choices. The examples cover most situations. I have also included strategies for special situations. Use these examples along with all the analytical tools you have learned in this book to make your own allocation decisions.

Let's use Joe for our first example. Joe is 35 years old and has just started working for Tank's R Us, a large industrial corporation. This is his first opportunity to invest in a 401(k) plan. His plan offers the three core investment options along with a company stock fund. He has an S&P 500 index fund called the Diversified Stock Fund, a bond index fund which has performed about the same as the Lehman Brothers Bond Aggregate index, and a money market account that has tracked the T-Bill rate. Joe knows he is investing for the long haul. His investment objective is to obtain maximum growth. He has about 30 years until retirement so he is not concerned with short-term stability of principle.

Based on his investment objective, Joe's decision is to invest all his 401(k) savings in the S&P 500 index fund. As Joe gets closer to retirement and his account value gets very large, he will likely move some of his contributions into the bond or money market fund. This will help to reduce fluctuations in principle. Outside his 401(k), Joe will save short-term money in a money market account in order to provide for emergencies.

Jill & Beth are office mates at ABC Corp. They are both 30 years old and plan to retire at 65. Since they have 35 years until retirement, they elect to invest all their 401(k) contributions in equities. This case is similar to Joe's, but Jill and Beth have more investment options to chose from. Table 7.3 shows the investment options available they have to choose from. There is a total of seven.

If you look at Table 7.3 you can see that the aggressive growth and world funds have performed very well within their respective categories. Growth Fund A has lagged far behind its category over the years. Growth Fund B was just recently added and does not have a long enough performance history with which to make a good decision.

Plan rules allow employees at ABC Corp. to make contributions in 5 percent increments to any combination of funds they desire. Jill chooses to allocate 60 percent of her money to the S&P 500 index fund, 20 percent to the worldwide fund, and 20 percent to the aggressive growth fund. Beth's choice is a little different. She chooses to allocate 40 percent to the S&P 500 fund, 30 percent to the aggressive growth fund and 30 percent to the foreign fund.

Jill and Beth both desire long-term growth, but notice that they both avoided funds in the growth category because the options do not seem to be winners. Instead, Jill and Beth both selected the best performing funds available. They didn't contribute to any fund severely lagging its category average. They plan to watch the newly added Growth Fund B to see how it performs over the next several years. If the fund shows good perfor-

Table 7.3   Real-Life 401(k) Investment Options

	1995	1994	1993	1992	1991	3 YR	5 YR	10 YR
Worldwide Fund	23.91	3.05	25.60	8.50	22.50	17.05	16.34	16.83
MSCI EAFE	*11.21*	*7.78*	*32.56*	*-12.17*	*12.13*	*16.69*	*9.37*	*13.62*
MSCI World	*20.72*	*5.08*	*22.50*	*-5.22*	*18.28*	*15.83*	*11.74*	*13.09*
Aggressive Growth Fund	39.00	-3.00	22.00	12.00	73.00	18.05	26.09	17.59
Aggressive Growth Category	*33.49*	*-3.08*	*19.38*	*9.19*	*54.81*	*15.59*	*21.16*	*14.17*
NASDAQ Composite	*39.92*	*-3.20*	*14.75*	*15.45*	*56.84*	*17.10*	*23.79*	*12.84*
Growth Fund A	22.00	-2.08	5.04	-1.09	28.87	7.86	9.85	9.75
Growth Fund B	26.00	n/a	n/a	n/a	n/a	n/a	n/a	n/a
Growth Category	*30.94*	*-1.82*	*11.78*	*8.50*	*37.61*	*12.85*	*16.50*	*13.54*
S&P 500	*37.53*	*1.31*	*10.06*	*7.70*	*30.33*	*15.32*	*16.57*	*14.84*
Balanced	23.00	-1.50	14.75	8.00	27.00	11.61	13.78	17.08
Balanced Category	*24.80*	*-2.81*	*13.40*	*7.05*	*26.44*	*11.21*	*13.24*	*11.43*
Intermediate Bond	14.50	-4.70	11.35	6.50	14.50	8.97	9.84	7.91
LB Aggregate	*18.47*	*-2.92*	*9.75*	*7.24*	*16.00*	*8.07*	*9.44*	*9.61*
T-Bills	*5.51*	*4.27*	*3.02*	*3.46*	*5.41*	*4.26*	*4.33*	*5.55*

This table shows a real-life example of the types of options available in a 401(k) plan. Jill and Beth are used as the example.
Indexes and category averages are in italic. Keep in mind that every plan is different. Use this as an example.

mance they may contribute part of their money to it without moving money out of existing funds. This will help to further diversify their portfolio.

Let me point out that there is no right or wrong allocation for Jill and Beth. An allocation of 100 percent in the index equity fund may end up doing just as well over the next 35 years. The allocation they did select allows diversification among different funds with a growth objective. It also allows them to take a little more risk in an effort to achieve a higher return.

Let's look at a third example. Jay is 60 and plans to retire at 65. He works for the same company as Jill and Beth. Jay has already accumulated a good nest egg through equity investments in his 401(k) plan. He plans to use the money in his 401(k) account to generate income during retirement. Jay's objective is to increase stability of principle in his account over the next five years. His decision is to transition from a growth allocation to a more income orientated allocation.

Jay's current allocation is 100 percent equities; 50 percent in the index fund, 25 percent in the world fund and 25 percent in the aggressive growth fund. Jay wants to generate current income in five years, but he still wants his nest egg to grow for 20 years or so during retirement. He also wants to continue benefiting from tax-deferred contributions into his account. His decision is to transition into 50 percent stocks, 40 percent bonds, and 10 percent money market over the next five years. He will gradually move money out of his aggressive growth fund and index equity fund into the balanced and bond funds. All future contributions will be made to the balanced, bond, and money market accounts. This allocation will help Jay achieve a good combination of price stability, current income and growth.

Now let's look at Bob. Bob works with Jay. He also plans to retire in five years when he hits 65, but Bob does not plan to use his 401(k) money at retirement. Bob's objective is to continue long-term growth. He is not concerned about short-term stability of principle. His plan is to leave his money in the 401(k) plan and let it grow. Bob is invested 80 percent equities and 20 percent in the balanced fund. He plans on maintaining his present allocation of 40 percent in the index fund, 20 percent foreign fund, and 20 percent aggressive growth fund, and 20 percent in the balanced fund.

The examples are very basic and only intended to show some possibilities. Remember, there are no right or wrong answers. You have your own wants, needs and desires, not to mention risk and comfort level. Hindsight has always been the best way to invest. Don't beat yourself up for not picking the fund that performed the best last year or for selecting a fund that experienced a down year. Analyze your objectives and investment options, then make your selections based upon the best information you have. Let time and the financial markets work to your advantage.

Remember, past performance does not guarantee future results. There is *never* a guaranteed return on any investment. Investing in any financial product involves some type of risk. It does not matter if you are in equities, bonds or cash equivalents. Risk is always an influencing factor when investing.

Strategies for Dual Income Families

If you and your spouse work and both have access to a 401(k), then there are some special strategies you may want to consider. If you both work for the same company then you basically have one plan in which you can put in more money. There is not much difference here. Be sure you both contribute enough to receive any matching funds. If your plans are different, then your strategies need to be expanded.

Start by gathering all the information available on both plans. Remember that each 401(k) plan has its own features. Build a performance worksheet for each plan using the worksheets in Table 7.1 and Table 7.2, then decide on your overall asset allocation plan. Look at the investment options among the two plans as one big candy store. Choose the best funds from each plan.

With two 401(k) plans to work with, you have the opportunity to dramatically increase the amount of matching contributions you receive. Make sure you both contribute enough to get the full matching contributions if they are available. It is also very helpful to contribute as much pre-tax money as you can. When you have two plans to choose from try to put as much pre-tax money as you can into the plan with the best options.

Let's look at another example. Remember Joe from Tanks R Us and Jill from ABC Corp.? In this example, they get married. Both can contribute $3,000 to their 401(k) and receive an equal match of $3,000 which gives a combined total of $12,000. They can both contribute another unmatched $3,000 to their plans. This money is tax-deferred. Their long-term objective for growth remains the same. Since Joe has only an S&P 500 index fund available in the equity category, he has no choice for a different allocation, but Jill can move her money into something that offers more diversification, plus the opportunity for higher returns. Instead of continually contributing to the index fund, Jill decides to move her future contributions into a split between the foreign and aggressive growth funds. This creates a combined portfolio of 50 percent in the S&P 500 index, 25 percent in aggressive growth, and 25 percent in a foreign fund. Of course as the funds grow the actual percentage values will change.

Joe and Jill also decide to contribute another $3,000 of unmatched pre-tax salary into their plans. Since Jill has the best growth options available, they decide to contribute the entire amount to Jill's plan. The money will go into the aggressive growth and world funds in an effort to achieve higher long-term returns. They will contribute money to a money market account outside of their 401(k) plans. As they get caught up with their wedding bills, Joe will contribute unmatched pre-tax money into his account. This allows a nice tax deduction while building a large retirement fund.

Strategies When Matching Employer Contributions Are Not Available

If your company offers a 401(k) plan but does not match your contributions, there are alternative strategies to consider. Even without the match, the 401(k) is still the best retirement vehicle available because you can contribute pre-tax money that will grow tax deferred until you withdraw it. With the exception of the IRA for certain income earners, there is no other investment vehicle in the world that can give you this double deferral opportunity. As long as your investment selection in the 401(k) plan is suitable, this is your best investment opportunity.

The only time I have seen better investment opportunities outside a 401(k) is when a plan is set up as a variable annuity contract. This is a common arrangement for 403(b) plans and it is sometimes found in a 401(k) plan. If you fall into this category, be sure to read the special section in Appendix C.

Strategies When Eligible for IRA Tax Deductions

If you are investing in a 401(k) and are eligible for a tax deductible IRA there are some strategies you can implement that may help in your investment options. Of course you should always contribute enough into your 401(k) to receive the maximum matching funds. If you have the opportunity to make unmatched pre-tax contributions into your 401(k) and you are eligible to make deductible contributions to an IRA, then there are a few things to consider.

First, take a look at the 401(k) investment options available. Are there enough options to meet your investment goals? If not, a self-directed IRA set up though a discount broker or directly with a no-load mutual fund family will allow you more diversification and possibly access to better equity funds. If you decide to go with the IRA, make sure you are familiar with mutual fund selection. If you have to go to a financial planner or full-service broker to select a mutual fund, you will end up spending more in hidden expenses than it's worth. If this is the case, stay with your 401(k) plan.

Where to Go for More Help

The National Association of 401(k) Investors (NA4I) is a nonprofit organization that teaches people how to invest in 401(k) and similar retirement benefits. Members receive a one-year subscription to the *401(k) Journal,* unlimited use of a Q&A Infoline and either a free copy of this book (valued at $19.95) or two free reports, "What to Do With Your Retirement Account When You Leave the Company" and "All About Self-Directed IRA Investing" (a total value of $24.00). You also get discounts on other information sources including a professionally prepared analysis of your own 401(k) investments. Membership dues are $39 per year. Your money goes a long way.

NA4I is independent of any other organization and accepts no advertising or endorsement revenues from outside sources. Beginning and advanced 401(k) investors are invited to join as are those who have similar retirement plans such as the 403(b), 457, Thrift Savings Plan for federal employees, SAR-SEP, and SIMPLE plans. To join, send a check or money order for $39 to **National Association of 401(k) Investors, Membership Services, P.O. Box 410755, Melbourne, FL 32941.** Be sure to indicate whether you want a copy of this book or the two information reports as part of your membership. For more information, call **(407) 636-5737.**

Chapter 8

What to Do With Your Account When You Leave the Company

When employment with your company ends, you need to know the options available for handling your 401(k) account. Several situations could trigger this event: the plan is terminated by your employer, you reach 59 1/2 years of age, you retire, resign, are laid off, or fired, you become disabled, or you die and your spouse is left with the account.

If any of these life-changing events happen, you have three general options with regard to processing your 401(k) account. The first option is to leave your account invested in the company 401(k) plan. The second option is to take a lump sum distribution. There are actually several options that fall into this category and we will discuss them later in the chapter. Your third option is to withdraw your money, pay a 10 percent penalty and pay ordinary income taxes if you are under 59 1/2 years of age.

Option 1: Leave Your Account With Your Employer

If you leave your company prior to normal retirement age, you have the right to maintain your 401(k) account with that employer if your vested account size is greater than $3,500. Your employer can not cash you out of the plan without your consent unless your account value is less than $3,500.

Leaving your 401(k) money with your former employer either permanently or temporarily can be an excellent choice. Your account will continue to grow in a low-cost investment vehicle. If you choose this route, you will still be able to roll your money into a new employer's plan or you can receive a lump sum distribution at a later time. The employer may place a restriction on how long these two options are available. If you pass the time limit, your account may be frozen in place until you turn 59 1/2.

If you decide to leave your money where it's at, you will need to find out how the employer handles certain activities. First, find out if you can take a lump sum distribution at any time after you leave or if the employer imposes a time limit. Most companies allow you to take a lump sum distribution at any time. But remember that some employers impose a time limit, after which you must wait until you are 59 1/2. If this is the case, you are probably better off rolling your 401(k) into an IRA so that you can maintain control.

Second, find out if there are any restrictions on the type of transactions you can make within your account. For example, you may not be allowed to transfer funds between different investment options. Also, find out if you will continue to receive all the information available for your 401(k) account. You need to keep informed of any changes or additions. Most employers will give you the same options you had when you were an employee except you won't be able to take loans or make contributions to your account.

If you are retiring, your employer may allow you to leave your account invested in the 401(k) while you receive monthly distributions. This is an excellent option because you can keep your money in familiar, low-cost investments. Most 401(k) plans do not charge loads or 12b-1 fees that are common with brokers and financial planners who sell investment products.

The disadvantage to leaving your money in the 401(k) after you retire is that your investment choices are limited to whatever funds are available in the plan. If you are not sure what to do with your money, you are probably better off leaving it where it is. This gives you time to educate yourself and learn your options. You are taking a very big risk by blindly turning your money over to someone else to manage. It is also risky to take the advice of someone who may not have your best interests in mind. Once again, ask your benefits office for information about leaving your 401(k) plan with the company when you retire. Let's summarize the advantages to leaving your 401(k) account with your employer after you leave the company:

- You can continue taking advantage of low cost 401(k) investing.
- You can stick with investments that you are familiar with.
- You can continue investing tax deferred.
- You can avoid the process of setting up an IRA and making investment selections at a time when you are under emotional stress.
- You can still roll your account into another employer's 401(k) if the new employer accept rollovers.
- You can still take a lump sum distribution in the future although certain company restrictions may apply.

Here are the disadvantages:

- Your investment selection is limited to plan options.
- Your old 401(k) plan may be structured as a variable annuity (see Appendix C).

Option 2: Take a Lump sum Distribution

The second choice you have when deciding what to do with your 401(k) account when you leave the company is to receive a lump sum distribution. There are two options available that allow you to continue tax deferral or allow you to take tax favored distributions. The first is to roll your money into another tax-qualified account and continue tax deferred investing. A qualified account is another 401(k) or an IRA. The second option is only available if you are 59 1/2 or older. It involves applying special tax forwarding averages to determine how much tax you pay on your lump sum distribution. When taking your lump sum distribution, you must take the entire account balance at once, regardless of which distribution option you choose. You cannot take some and leave some.

How to Roll Your Account Into a Qualified Plan

You can maintain tax-deferred investing by rolling your lump sum distribution into another qualified account. As mentioned earlier, this can be either an IRA or another employer's 401(k) plan. If your account contains contributions that were made after-tax, then not all of your money is eligible for the rollover. Only pre-tax contributions made by you or on your behalf are eligible. Any after-tax contributions can not be rolled over.

When taking a distribution for rollover purposes, there are two methods available to process the transaction. The first method is the *direct rollover*, and the second method is called the *rollover paid to you*. There is a very big difference between the two methods. Be sure to read the next few paragraphs very carefully.

Direct Rollover

A **direct rollover** is when your new plan trustee receives your money directly from the original agent. Your entire account is rolled over. There are no withholding taxes deducted and you can continue tax deferred investing. This is the best method for moving your 401(k) account to your new employer or to an IRA because all of your money is transferred, you avoid with-holding taxes, and your tax deferral status is preserved.

To make a direct rollover, you must coordinate the transfer between the current trustee and the new one. This is easy to do. Once you select your new trustee, request that they set up your new account as well as the actual transfer. The current trustee will contact you and have you sign some papers. The account will be distributed as you requested. A check will be issued to your new trustee "for benefit of" (FBO) you. This prevents you from getting control of the money and using it outside a qualified retirement account. Only your trustee can deposit the check into your account.

Use the direct rollover when transferring your money to a qualified account.

Rollover Paid to You

The rules for rollovers of a 401(k) account have changed. In the past you could receive your account value and do anything you wanted with the money for up to 60 days. Before the end of the 60 days, you had to put the money in a tax-qualified plan or suffer the tax consequences.

Today things are different. In a **rollover paid to you** your account is liquidated and the money is sent to you less 20 percent which is withheld for income taxes. You have 60 days to put the money you received into a tax qualified plan. If you only deposit the 80 percent of your account, then the 20 percent that was withheld for taxes is considered a withdrawal. You must then pay a 10 percent penalty and any additional taxes due depending on your tax bracket.

You can get the 20 percent that was withheld back by coming up with the money out of your own pocket and depositing it into the qualified plan with the other 80 percent within the sixty-day period. You will then get your 20 percent back when you file your income tax return.

The rollover paid to you is a difficult way to transfer your account. Suppose your account is worth $100,000 and $20,000 is withheld. It is your responsibility to come up with $20,000 to replace the withheld money or face severe tax consequences. If you're like most people, it may be very difficult to come up with the additional $20,000. Even if you do have access to the money, I bet you can think of a hundred other things to do with the money than to tie it up until you get your tax refund.

Do not use a rollover paid to you! Use a direct rollover.

The terminology used when discussing account transfers can be confusing. Some people refer to both methods as simply a *rollover*. Don't worry about the terminology. Just make sure that the transfer is set up so that you do not get access to the money at any point during the transaction. This means that the check should be made out "For Benefit of You".

Option 2a: Roll Your Account Into Your New Employer's 401(k)

If you are moving on to a new employer who also has a 401(k) plan, you may have the option to roll your money into the new plan (assuming the new employer accepts rollovers). By doing this, you receive several benefits. First of all, you maintain low-cost, tax-deferred investing. You will also have funds available for loans and you preserve special forward averaging tax options for when you turn 59 1/2 and take a distribution from your account.

The disadvantage of rolling your money into the new plan is that your investment options are limited to whatever the new employer offers. If the options available with your former employer are good, it might be a good idea to maintain your account instead of moving it to the new plan. You can then start another account with the new employer. The disadvantage is that you will have more statements to track and you will not be able to get a loan from the account with your previous employer.

Some 401(k) accounts have excellent investment options. I have seen some arranged with mutual fund companies such as Fidelity that offer a wide selection of some of the best performing funds available. On the other hand, some 401(k) plans have only a limited selection.

It is important to note that if you roll over your account to a brokerage house or financial planner your investment choices will also be limited. You are restricted to whatever basket of products they sell for a commission. You will likely be saddled with either a front- or back-end sales load and a 12b-1 fee. Not only is this an expensive alternative, but the options available may not be as good as the ones available in either the new or the old 401(k) plan. Just because the salesperson has a very large quantity of products to choose from does not mean that the quality of their selection is better.

I have seen people roll their money over to a financial consultant after hearing about getting access to hundreds of funds that will make them rich. Too many times these funds provide a smaller return than the few options available within the 401(k) plan. Now, let's review the advantages and disadvantages of rolling your money into another employer's 401(k).

Advantages
- You can continue taking advantage of the low costs associated with 401(k) investing.
- You can continue investing tax deferred.
- You have funds available for loans.
- You preserve special forward averaging tax options for when you turn 59 1/2 and take a distribution from your account. New legislation, however, is phasing out these options. More on this later.

Disadvantages
- Your investment selection is limited to plan options.
- Your account must typically remain with the new employer until you leave the company.
- Your new plan may be structured as a variable annuity (see Appendix C).

Option 2b: Roll Your Account Into an IRA

The rollover to a self-directed IRA is a great way to diversify your retirement investments. It allows you to pursue investment types that are not available inside your 401(k) plan. There are both advantages and disadvantages to the IRA option.

Advantages
- You have an increased amount of options to choose from.
- You can diversify your investments.
- You have access to funds with potentially higher returns.
- You can move your money whenever you want.

Disadvantages
- You cannot make loans from an IRA.
- You are not eligible for special forward averaging tax provisions that can reduce your tax burden when you retire.

- You may end up in poor performing investments if you are not educated on investing.
- You may end up with high commission investments if you work through a financial salesperson.

Conduit IRA

A **conduit IRA** is an IRA account containing only your roll-over money. You do not contribute funds from any other source into it. The IRA acts as a conduit between your past employer and your future employer. By rolling your 401(k) account into a conduit IRA, you preserve your ability to roll your money into a future employer's 401(k) plan.

When you set up a conduit IRA, you will need to select an investment to put your money into. If you purchase mutual funds via a broker, financial consultant, bank, or other financial salesperson you will end up paying either a front-end or a back-end sales load. This expense will take a big chunk out of your account value.

Most financial salespersons will set you up with a back-end sales load or deferred sales fee as it is sometimes called. The deferred sales fee usually declines to zero over a seven-year period. This prevents you from moving your account prior to the company reimbursing itself for commissions paid to the salesperson. The company does this by collecting a hidden 12b-1 fee from your account. If you plan on rolling over your 401(k) lump sum distribution to a conduit IRA and later to another employer's 401(k) plan, you may pay a steep price in front end loads or deferred sales fees if your IRA is set up by a financial salesperson.

To avoid heavy sales fees, you should select no-load mutual funds on your own through a self-directed conduit IRA. If you are uncomfortable doing this, than you will probably be better off rolling your account directly to your new employer's 401(k) plan. Rolling over your 401(k) into an IRA gives you more control over your money and provides the opportunity to build wealth. Just make sure you know how to select no-load mutual funds before you execute this option.

Option 2c: Withdraw You Funds Using Five- and Ten-Year Forward Averaging

If you are 59 1/2 years or older you are eligible for special forward averaging methods that may reduce your tax liability when you receive your lump sum distribution. With these methods you can withdraw your entire account and possibly pay a lower tax then if you were to take periodic distributions.

There are two different methods of averaging. The first is called the *five-year averaging method*. The second is called the *ten-year averaging method*. If you were born prior to 1936 you can use either method. If you were born after 1936 and are 59 1/2 or older you are only eligible for the five-year method.

The forward averaging methods we are talking about allow you to calculate taxes owed on your lump sum distribution as if you were receiving equally distributed payments over a five- or ten-year period. The tax liability can be less than you would pay if you took normal distributions during retirement. By using one of these averaging methods, you may be able to get all of your money out of the 401(k) account at a reduced tax rate.

The forward averaging method can only be used once in a lifetime and is applied to your entire distribution. You cannot roll over a portion of your lump sum and apply the forward averaging to the remaining amount. It is all or nothing. If you roll your account into an IRA, you lose the opportunity to apply the forward averaging in the future. The exception is if you use a conduit IRA and later roll it into anther 401(k) plan. The total tax on your lump sum is due the first year you receive your distribution when you apply forward averaging. 403(b) and Federal Thrift Savings Plans are not eligible for forward averaging.

The topic of how to calculate the five- and ten-year averaging methods is some what involved (as well as lengthy), so it is beyond the scope of this book to include it here. At this point it is more important for you to know that the method exists than to be able to perform the calculations in detail.

New legislation eliminates the five-year forward averaging method after 1999. Ten-year averaging remains available for those who were born prior to 1936. As you can see, the legislation phases out both forward averaging methods over time.

Let's review the advantages and disadvantages of using the special forward averaging methods to calculate taxes owed on your lump sum distribution.

Advantages
- You may pay a lower tax on the entire distribution.
- Forward averaging usually is most beneficial to individuals who have account values less than $400,000, plan on using the money in the near term, and are in the 28 percent or higher tax bracket.

Disadvantages
- You must withdraw the entire account to apply the forward averaging.
- You may only use this option once in a lifetime.

Option 3: Withdraw Your Money and Pay Heavy Penalties

This third option for how to handle your 401(k) account after you leave the company is to receive all your money from your account and not apply any of the previous options. Your entire distribution is considered income for that year and taxed as ordinary income. You must also pay a 10 percent penalty if you are under 59 1/2 years of age. After working so hard to accumulate the money in your account, it's a shame to lose so much of it to penalties and taxes.

If you are less than 59 1/2 years old, you can roll over your lump sum distribution into an IRA and start taking distributions that are not subject to penalties. This is helpful if you plan to retire early. Of course there are certain restrictions and special methods used to calculate your distributions.

Summary

When employment with your company ends, you have many options available for how to handle your 401(k) account. Each option has advantages and disadvantages. Use the chart in Table 8.1 as an overview.

How To Build Wealth With Your 401(k)

Table 8.1   401(k) Options When You Leave the Company

Options	Conditions	Advantages	Disadvantages
Leave your 401(k) account with your employer.	Your account must be greater than $3,500 or else your employer may cash you out.	• You can continue low cost 401(k) investing. • You can stick with investments that you are familiar with. • You can continue investing tax deferred. • You can avoid the process of setting up an IRA and making investment selections at a time when you are under emotional stress. • You can roll your account into another employer's 401(k) at a later time if the new employer accepts rollovers. • You can take a lump sum distribution at some time in the future although certain company restrictions may apply.	• Your investment selection is limited to plan options. • Your previous employer's 401(k) plan may be structured as a variable annuity. (see Appendix C).
Roll your account into another employer's 401(k) account.	The new employer must have a 401(k) account and must accept transfers.	• You can continue low cost 401(k) investing. • You can continue investing tax deferred. • You have funds available for loans. • You preserve special forward averaging tax options when you turn 59 1/2 and take a distribution from your account (these options are being phased out).	• Your investment selection is limited to plan options. • Typically, your account must remain with the new employer until you leave the company. • The new plan may be structured as a variable annuity. (see Appendix C).
Roll your account into an IRA or a conduit IRA.	Only pre-tax contributions can be rolled over.	• You have an increased amount of options to choose from. • You can diversify your investments. • You have access to funds with potentially higher returns. • You can move your money at any time.	• You can't get loans from an IRA. • You are not eligible for special forward averaging tax provisions that can reduce your tax burden when you retire. • You may end up in poor performing investments if you are not educated on investing. • You may end up with high commission investments if you work through a financial salesperson.
Apply a five- or ten-year averaging method to calculate taxes due on lump sum distribution.	If you were born prior to 1936 you can use either the 5 or 10 year method. If you were born after 1936 and are 59 1/2 or older, you can only use the 5 year method.	• You may pay a lower tax on the entire distribution. • Forward averaging usually is most beneficial to individuals who have account values less than $400,000, plan on using the money in the near term, and are in the 28 percent or higher tax bracket.	• You must withdraw the entire account to apply the forward averaging. • You may only use this option once in a lifetime
Withdraw the money and pay taxes and penalties.	None.	• Immediate access to the money.	• You pay ordinary income taxes, plus a 10 percent penalty if you are under 59 1/2 years of age.

Chapter 9

Bottom Line Wealth Building Strategies

1 Invest Tax Deferred

Tax-deferred investing is a very powerful financial leveraging tool. It allows you to accumulate a very large sum of money over time because you have extra money working for you. You are essentially borrowing money by not paying taxes on it. The borrowed money is invested so that the power of compounding interest is working in your favor. Although you will eventually owe taxes on the deferred amount, your investment will grow exponentially and you will have much more money than you need when it comes time to finally pay the taxes. Tax deferred investing, coupled with the power of compound interest, has made many people wealthy over time.

A word of caution. Make sure you don't try so hard to avoid taxes that you forget about making money. Many tax avoidance investments turn out to be losers or have such high hidden fees that their performance is worse than a taxable investment. Examples include limited partnerships, whole or universal life insurance and many variable annuities.

401(k) investing is a wonderful way to enjoy low cost, tax deferred investing. Not only are your contributions tax deferred, but your investments also *grow* tax deferred. This double deferment is very powerful in accumulating wealth.

With the exception of the IRA, and only in certain cases, no other tax-deferred vehicle like this is available.

In addition to double deferment, almost all 401(k) investors enjoy low cost investing which allows you to achieve good gains without the burden of hidden fees, loads and commissions. It is wise to contribute the highest level of pre-tax contributions you are allowed to make as soon as you are eligible to participate in the plan. This gives you an immediate tax benefit along with more money available to earn compound interest

There are three main reasons why you should not delay contributing pre-tax dollars to your 401(k). First, tax laws may change and reduce or even eliminate the ability to make pre-tax contributions. Second, your contribution level may become restricted due to legislation forcing your employer to meet certain discrimination criteria. If you wait until you think you can afford it, you may not be eligible to contribute as much or even any at all. And third, by delaying your contributions, you lose the advantage of growth over time.

2 Employ a Long Time Horizon

Investing must have a long time horizon. The longer you have to invest, the more exponential the effects of compounding interest become. You must allow time for the fluctuations in the financial markets to smooth themselves out. You may remember from earlier discussions that the stock market as measured by the S&P 500 over a 60-year period had a negative annual return 26 percent of the time. Yet, it still returned an average 12 percent annually over the entire 60-year time frame. Think long term when investing. Don't panic when the financial markets slide for short periods of time. One or two years is considered a short period of time when it comes to investing.

Your 401(k) is a retirement investing vehicle which inherently makes it an investment for the long term. Use it to your advantage. Do not access funds in the plan until retirement. The longer you have until retirement, the wealthier you will become as the result of your 401(k) investments.

3 Use Systematic Investing

Systematic investing is another technique used to amass great wealth. You will probably not have a large sum of money to invest at one time, but a continual investment of small amounts of money will enable you to build up significant wealth over time. Systematic investing also reduces your risk of buying at higher prices. Using a systematic approach means you will buy more shares when market prices are low and less when prices are high.

You automatically get systematic investing when you invest through your 401(k) plan. Contributions are deducted from your paycheck before you have the chance to spend them on something less important. You free yourself from worry when the markets temporarily drop and when the crisis of the month has everyone else panicking. When the markets are down, think about how many shares you are buying at a discounted price.

4 Buy and Hold Your Funds

Individuals who have become wealthy by investing employ a disciplined approach of buying and holding their investments. If you trade investments every year or two, then you are speculating and not investing. As an investor you must allow time for your funds to grow. This way you can ride out fluctuations in the financial markets. Studies show that investors who time the market, or chase last year's hottest investments, typically have a lower long-term return than those who invest and hold their positions.

Take your clue from this research. A good fund will continually meet or beat its category average. Let your fund managers buy and sell securities within the funds you own. Don't try to second guess what the fund will return. This is the job of the fund manager you have hired. If you choose a good fund, then you will reap the benefits of good returns over time. If you don't feel comfortable with any of the managed equity funds available in your plan, then get into an index fund if available.

5 Maximize Returns Don't Minimize Risks

You must assume some risk in order to achieve higher returns. Many novice investors try to protect capital by placing it in "safe" low return investments such as money market and fixed-income funds. They purposely avoid stocks with large price variations. This is a mistake. If you employ this false logic, you will lose money to inflation over time. Concentrate on maximizing gains, not minimizing risks.

When investing within your 401(k), it is better to plan for the long term by purchasing equities than playing it safe in bonds and money market funds. A 401(k) investment should seek growth of investments, not short-term avoidance of negative returns.

6 Invest Early, Often and Wisely!

This is the best advice you can receive. Start your 401(k) as soon as you can. Contribute to it with every paycheck. And use all the information you have learned in this book to make the most informed investment decisions!

APPENDIX A

Present and Future Value Tables

Appendix A-1 Future Value of a Single Payment

Years	1%	2%	3%	4%	5%	6%	7%	8%	9%
1	1.010	1.020	1.030	1.040	1.050	1.060	1.070	1.080	1.090
2	1.020	1.040	1.061	1.082	1.103	1.124	1.145	1.166	1.188
3	1.030	1.061	1.093	1.125	1.158	1.191	1.225	1.260	1.295
4	1.041	1.082	1.126	1.170	1.216	1.262	1.311	1.360	1.412
5	1.051	1.104	1.159	1.217	1.276	1.338	1.403	1.469	1.539
6	1.062	1.126	1.194	1.265	1.340	1.419	1.501	1.587	1.677
7	1.072	1.149	1.230	1.316	1.407	1.504	1.606	1.714	1.828
8	1.083	1.172	1.267	1.369	1.477	1.594	1.718	1.851	1.993
9	1.094	1.195	1.305	1.423	1.551	1.689	1.838	1.999	2.172
10	1.105	1.219	1.344	1.480	1.629	1.791	1.967	2.159	2.367
11	1.116	1.243	1.384	1.539	1.710	1.898	2.105	2.332	2.580
12	1.127	1.268	1.426	1.601	1.796	2.012	2.252	2.518	2.813
13	1.138	1.294	1.469	1.665	1.886	2.133	2.410	2.720	3.066
14	1.149	1.319	1.513	1.732	1.980	2.261	2.579	2.937	3.342
15	1.161	1.346	1.558	1.801	2.079	2.397	2.759	3.172	3.642
16	1.173	1.373	1.605	1.873	2.183	2.540	2.952	3.426	3.970
17	1.184	1.400	1.653	1.948	2.292	2.693	3.159	3.700	4.328
18	1.196	1.428	1.702	2.026	2.407	2.854	3.380	3.996	4.717
19	1.208	1.457	1.754	2.107	2.527	3.026	3.617	4.316	5.142
20	1.220	1.486	1.806	2.191	2.653	3.207	3.870	4.661	5.604
21	1.232	1.516	1.860	2.279	2.786	3.400	4.141	5.034	6.109
22	1.245	1.546	1.916	2.370	2.925	3.604	4.430	5.437	6.659
23	1.257	1.577	1.974	2.465	3.072	3.820	4.741	5.871	7.258
24	1.270	1.608	2.033	2.563	3.225	4.049	5.072	6.341	7.911
25	1.282	1.641	2.094	2.666	3.386	4.292	5.427	6.848	8.623
26	1.295	1.673	2.157	2.772	3.556	4.549	5.807	7.396	9.399
27	1.308	1.707	2.221	2.883	3.733	4.822	6.214	7.988	10.245
28	1.321	1.741	2.288	2.999	3.920	5.112	6.649	8.627	11.167
29	1.335	1.776	2.357	3.119	4.116	5.418	7.114	9.317	12.172
30	1.348	1.811	2.427	3.243	4.322	5.743	7.612	10.063	13.268
31	1.361	1.848	2.500	3.373	4.538	6.088	8.145	10.868	14.462
32	1.375	1.885	2.575	3.508	4.765	6.453	8.715	11.737	15.763
33	1.389	1.922	2.652	3.648	5.003	6.841	9.325	12.676	17.182
34	1.403	1.961	2.732	3.794	5.253	7.251	9.978	13.690	18.728
35	1.417	2.000	2.814	3.946	5.516	7.686	10.677	14.785	20.414
40	1.489	2.208	3.262	4.801	7.040	10.286	14.974	21.725	31.409
45	1.565	2.438	3.782	5.841	8.985	13.765	21.002	31.920	48.327
50	1.645	2.692	4.384	7.107	11.467	18.420	29.457	46.902	74.358
55	1.729	2.972	5.082	8.646	14.636	24.650	41.315	68.914	114.408
60	1.817	3.281	5.892	10.520	18.679	32.988	57.946	101.257	176.031

How to Build Wealth With Your 401(k)

Appendix A-1 Future Value of a Single Payment

Years	10%	12%	14%	15%	16%	18%	20%	25%	30%
1	1.100	1.120	1.140	1.150	1.160	1.180	1.200	1.250	1.300
2	1.210	1.254	1.300	1.323	1.346	1.392	1.440	1.563	1.690
3	1.331	1.405	1.482	1.521	1.561	1.643	1.728	1.953	2.197
4	1.464	1.574	1.689	1.749	1.811	1.939	2.074	2.441	2.856
5	1.611	1.762	1.925	2.011	2.100	2.288	2.488	3.052	3.713
6	1.772	1.974	2.195	2.313	2.436	2.700	2.986	3.815	4.827
7	1.949	2.211	2.502	2.660	2.826	3.185	3.583	4.768	6.275
8	2.144	2.476	2.853	3.059	3.278	3.759	4.300	5.960	8.157
9	2.358	2.773	3.252	3.518	3.803	4.435	5.160	7.451	10.604
10	2.594	3.106	3.707	4.046	4.411	5.234	6.192	9.313	13.786
11	2.853	3.479	4.226	4.652	5.117	6.176	7.430	11.642	17.922
12	3.138	3.896	4.818	5.350	5.936	7.288	8.916	14.552	23.298
13	3.452	4.363	5.492	6.153	6.886	8.599	10.699	18.190	30.288
14	3.797	4.887	6.261	7.076	7.988	10.147	12.839	22.737	39.374
15	4.177	5.474	7.138	8.137	9.266	11.974	15.407	28.422	51.186
16	4.595	6.130	8.137	9.358	10.748	14.129	18.488	35.527	66.542
17	5.054	6.866	9.276	10.761	12.468	16.672	22.186	44.409	86.504
18	5.560	7.690	10.575	12.375	14.463	19.673	26.623	55.511	112.455
19	6.116	8.613	12.056	14.232	16.777	23.214	31.948	69.389	146.192
20	6.727	9.646	13.743	16.367	19.461	27.393	38.338	86.736	190.050
21	7.400	10.804	15.668	18.822	22.574	32.324	46.005	108.420	247.065
22	8.140	12.100	17.861	21.645	26.186	38.142	55.206	135.525	321.184
23	8.954	13.552	20.362	24.891	30.376	45.008	66.247	169.407	417.539
24	9.850	15.179	23.212	28.625	35.236	53.109	79.497	211.758	542.801
25	10.835	17.000	26.462	32.919	40.874	62.669	95.396	264.698	705.641
26	11.918	19.040	30.167	37.857	47.414	73.949	114.475	330.872	917.333
27	13.110	21.325	34.390	43.535	55.000	87.260	137.371	413.590	1192.533
28	14.421	23.884	39.204	50.066	63.800	102.967	164.845	516.988	1550.293
29	15.863	26.750	44.693	57.575	74.009	121.501	197.814	646.235	2015.381
30	17.449	29.960	50.950	66.212	85.850	143.371	237.376	807.794	2619.996
31	19.194	33.555	58.083	76.144	99.586	169.177	284.852	1009.742	3405.994
32	21.114	37.582	66.215	87.565	115.520	199.629	341.822	1262.177	4427.793
33	23.225	42.092	75.485	100.700	134.003	235.563	410.186	1577.722	5756.130
34	25.548	47.143	86.053	115.805	155.443	277.964	492.224	1972.152	7482.970
35	28.102	52.800	98.100	133.176	180.314	327.997	590.668	2465.190	9727.860
40	45.259	93.051	188.884	267.864	378.721	750.378	1469.772	7523.164	36118.865
45	72.890	163.988	363.679	538.769	795.444	1716.684	3657.262	22958.874	134106.82
50	117.391	289.002	700.233	1083.657	1670.704	3927.357	9100.438	70064.923	497929.22
55	189.059	509.321	1348.239	2179.622	3509.049	8984.841	22644.802	213821.2	1848776.3
60	304.482	897.597	2595.919	4383.999	7370.201	20555.140	56347.514	652530.4	6864377.2

Appendix A-2 Future Value of an Annuity

Years	1%	2%	3%	4%	5%	6%	7%	8%	9%
1	1.000	1.000	1.000	1.000	1.000	1.000	1.000	1.000	1.000
2	2.010	2.020	2.030	2.040	2.050	2.060	2.070	2.080	2.090
3	3.030	3.060	3.091	3.122	3.153	3.184	3.215	3.246	3.278
4	4.060	4.122	4.184	4.246	4.310	4.375	4.440	4.506	4.573
5	5.101	5.204	5.309	5.416	5.526	5.637	5.751	5.867	5.985
6	6.152	6.308	6.468	6.633	6.802	6.975	7.153	7.336	7.523
7	7.214	7.434	7.662	7.898	8.142	8.394	8.654	8.923	9.200
8	8.286	8.583	8.892	9.214	9.549	9.897	10.260	10.637	11.028
9	9.369	9.755	10.159	10.583	11.027	11.491	11.978	12.488	13.021
10	10.462	10.950	11.464	12.006	12.578	13.181	13.816	14.487	15.193
11	11.567	12.169	12.808	13.486	14.207	14.972	15.784	16.645	17.560
12	12.683	13.412	14.192	15.026	15.917	16.870	17.888	18.977	20.141
13	13.809	14.680	15.618	16.627	17.713	18.882	20.141	21.495	22.953
14	14.947	15.974	17.086	18.292	19.599	21.015	22.550	24.215	26.019
15	16.097	17.293	18.599	20.024	21.579	23.276	25.129	27.152	29.361
16	17.258	18.639	20.157	21.825	23.657	25.673	27.888	30.324	33.003
17	18.430	20.012	21.762	23.698	25.840	28.213	30.840	33.750	36.974
18	19.615	21.412	23.414	25.645	28.132	30.906	33.999	37.450	41.301
19	20.811	22.841	25.117	27.671	30.539	33.760	37.379	41.446	46.018
20	22.019	24.297	26.870	29.778	33.066	36.786	40.995	45.762	51.160
21	23.239	25.783	28.676	31.969	35.719	39.993	44.865	50.423	56.765
22	24.472	27.299	30.537	34.248	38.505	43.392	49.006	55.457	62.873
23	25.716	28.845	32.453	36.618	41.430	46.996	53.436	60.893	69.532
24	26.973	30.422	34.426	39.083	44.502	50.816	58.177	66.765	76.790
25	28.243	32.030	36.459	41.646	47.727	54.865	63.249	73.106	84.701
26	29.526	33.671	38.553	44.312	51.113	59.156	68.676	79.954	93.324
27	30.821	35.344	40.710	47.084	54.669	63.706	74.484	87.351	102.723
28	32.129	37.051	42.931	49.968	58.403	68.528	80.698	95.339	112.968
29	33.450	38.792	45.219	52.966	62.323	73.640	87.347	103.966	124.135
30	34.785	40.568	47.575	56.085	66.439	79.058	94.461	113.283	136.308
31	36.133	42.379	50.003	59.328	70.761	84.802	102.073	123.346	149.575
32	37.494	44.227	52.503	62.701	75.299	90.890	110.218	134.214	164.037
33	38.869	46.112	55.078	66.210	80.064	97.343	118.933	145.951	179.800
34	40.258	48.034	57.730	69.858	85.067	104.184	128.259	158.627	196.982
35	41.660	49.994	60.462	73.652	90.320	111.435	138.237	172.317	215.711
40	48.886	60.402	75.401	95.026	120.800	154.762	199.635	259.057	337.882
45	56.481	71.893	92.720	121.029	159.700	212.744	285.749	386.506	525.859
50	64.463	84.579	112.797	152.667	209.348	290.336	406.529	573.770	815.084
55	72.852	98.587	136.072	191.159	272.713	394.172	575.929	848.923	1260.092
60	81.670	114.052	163.053	237.991	353.584	533.128	813.520	1253.213	1944.792

How to Build Wealth With Your 401(k)

Appendix A-2 Future Value of an Annuity

Years	10%	12%	14%	15%	16%	18%	20%	25%	30%
1	1.000	1.000	1.000	1.000	1.000	1.000	1.000	1.000	1.000
2	2.100	2.120	2.140	2.150	2.160	2.180	2.200	2.250	2.300
3	3.310	3.374	3.440	3.473	3.506	3.572	3.640	3.813	3.990
4	4.641	4.779	4.921	4.993	5.066	5.215	5.368	5.766	6.187
5	6.105	6.353	6.610	6.742	6.877	7.154	7.442	8.207	9.043
6	7.716	8.115	8.536	8.754	8.977	9.442	9.930	11.259	12.756
7	9.487	10.089	10.730	11.067	11.414	12.142	12.916	15.073	17.583
8	11.436	12.300	13.233	13.727	14.240	15.327	16.499	19.842	23.858
9	13.579	14.776	16.085	16.786	17.519	19.086	20.799	25.802	32.015
10	15.937	17.549	19.337	20.304	21.321	23.521	25.959	33.253	42.619
11	18.531	20.655	23.045	24.349	25.733	28.755	32.150	42.566	56.405
12	21.384	24.133	27.271	29.002	30.850	34.931	39.581	54.208	74.327
13	24.523	28.029	32.089	34.352	36.786	42.219	48.497	68.760	97.625
14	27.975	32.393	37.581	40.505	43.672	50.818	59.196	86.949	127.913
15	31.772	37.280	43.842	47.580	51.660	60.965	72.035	109.687	167.286
16	35.950	42.753	50.980	55.717	60.925	72.939	87.442	138.109	218.472
17	40.545	48.884	59.118	65.075	71.673	87.068	105.931	173.636	285.014
18	45.599	55.750	68.394	75.836	84.141	103.740	128.117	218.045	371.518
19	51.159	63.440	78.969	88.212	98.603	123.414	154.740	273.556	483.973
20	57.275	72.052	91.025	102.444	115.380	146.628	186.688	342.945	630.165
21	64.002	81.699	104.768	118.810	134.841	174.021	225.026	429.681	820.215
22	71.403	92.503	120.436	137.632	157.415	206.345	271.031	538.101	1067.280
23	79.543	104.603	138.297	159.276	183.601	244.487	326.237	673.626	1388.464
24	88.497	118.155	158.659	184.168	213.978	289.494	392.484	843.033	1806.003
25	98.347	133.334	181.871	212.793	249.214	342.603	471.981	1054.791	2348.803
26	109.182	150.334	208.333	245.712	290.088	405.272	567.377	1319.489	3054.444
27	121.100	169.374	238.499	283.569	337.502	479.221	681.853	1650.361	3971.778
28	134.210	190.699	272.889	327.104	392.503	566.481	819.223	2063.952	5164.311
29	148.631	214.583	312.094	377.170	456.303	669.447	984.068	2580.939	6714.604
30	164.494	241.333	356.787	434.745	530.312	790.948	1181.882	3227.174	8729.985
31	181.943	271.293	407.737	500.957	616.162	934.319	1419.258	4034.968	11349.981
32	201.138	304.848	465.820	577.100	715.747	1103.496	1704.109	5044.710	14755.975
33	222.252	342.429	532.035	664.666	831.267	1303.125	2045.931	6306.887	19183.768
34	245.477	384.521	607.520	765.365	965.270	1538.688	2456.118	7884.609	24939.899
35	271.024	431.663	693.573	881.170	1120.713	1816.652	2948.341	9856.761	32422.868
40	442.593	767.091	1342.025	1779.090	2360.757	4163.213	7343.858	30088.655	120392.9
45	718.905	1358.230	2590.565	3585.128	4965.274	9531.577	18281.310	91831.496	447019.4
50	1163.909	2400.018	4994.521	7217.716	10435.649	21813.094	45497.191	280255.69	1659760.7
55	1880.591	4236.005	9623.134	14524.148	21925.305	49910.228	113219.01	855280.71	6162584.5
60	3034.816	7471.641	18535.133	29219.992	46057.509	114189.7	281732.6	2610117.8	22881254

Appendix A-3 Present Value of a Single Payment

Years	1%	2%	3%	4%	5%	6%	7%	8%	9%
1	0.990	0.980	0.971	0.962	0.952	0.943	0.935	0.926	0.917
2	0.980	0.961	0.943	0.925	0.907	0.890	0.873	0.857	0.842
3	0.971	0.942	0.915	0.889	0.864	0.840	0.816	0.794	0.772
4	0.961	0.924	0.888	0.855	0.823	0.792	0.763	0.735	0.708
5	0.951	0.906	0.863	0.822	0.784	0.747	0.713	0.681	0.650
6	0.942	0.888	0.837	0.790	0.746	0.705	0.666	0.630	0.596
7	0.933	0.871	0.813	0.760	0.711	0.665	0.623	0.583	0.547
8	0.923	0.853	0.789	0.731	0.677	0.627	0.582	0.540	0.502
9	0.914	0.837	0.766	0.703	0.645	0.592	0.544	0.500	0.460
10	0.905	0.820	0.744	0.676	0.614	0.558	0.508	0.463	0.422
11	0.896	0.804	0.722	0.650	0.585	0.527	0.475	0.429	0.388
12	0.887	0.788	0.701	0.625	0.557	0.497	0.444	0.397	0.356
13	0.879	0.773	0.681	0.601	0.530	0.469	0.415	0.368	0.326
14	0.870	0.758	0.661	0.577	0.505	0.442	0.388	0.340	0.299
15	0.861	0.743	0.642	0.555	0.481	0.417	0.362	0.315	0.275
16	0.853	0.728	0.623	0.534	0.458	0.394	0.339	0.292	0.252
17	0.844	0.714	0.605	0.513	0.436	0.371	0.317	0.270	0.231
18	0.836	0.700	0.587	0.494	0.416	0.350	0.296	0.250	0.212
19	0.828	0.686	0.570	0.475	0.396	0.331	0.277	0.232	0.194
20	0.820	0.673	0.554	0.456	0.377	0.312	0.258	0.215	0.178
21	0.811	0.660	0.538	0.439	0.359	0.294	0.242	0.199	0.164
22	0.803	0.647	0.522	0.422	0.342	0.278	0.226	0.184	0.150
23	0.795	0.634	0.507	0.406	0.326	0.262	0.211	0.170	0.138
24	0.788	0.622	0.492	0.390	0.310	0.247	0.197	0.158	0.126
25	0.780	0.610	0.478	0.375	0.295	0.233	0.184	0.146	0.116
26	0.772	0.598	0.464	0.361	0.281	0.220	0.172	0.135	0.106
27	0.764	0.586	0.450	0.347	0.268	0.207	0.161	0.125	0.098
28	0.757	0.574	0.437	0.333	0.255	0.196	0.150	0.116	0.090
29	0.749	0.563	0.424	0.321	0.243	0.185	0.141	0.107	0.082
30	0.742	0.552	0.412	0.308	0.231	0.174	0.131	0.099	0.075
31	0.735	0.541	0.400	0.296	0.220	0.164	0.123	0.092	0.069
32	0.727	0.531	0.388	0.285	0.210	0.155	0.115	0.085	0.063
33	0.720	0.520	0.377	0.274	0.200	0.146	0.107	0.079	0.058
34	0.713	0.510	0.366	0.264	0.190	0.138	0.100	0.073	0.053
35	0.706	0.500	0.355	0.253	0.181	0.130	0.094	0.068	0.049
40	0.672	0.453	0.307	0.208	0.142	0.097	0.067	0.046	0.032
45	0.639	0.410	0.264	0.171	0.111	0.073	0.048	0.031	0.021
50	0.608	0.372	0.228	0.141	0.087	0.054	0.034	0.021	0.013
55	0.579	0.337	0.197	0.116	0.068	0.041	0.024	0.015	0.009
60	0.550	0.305	0.170	0.095	0.054	0.030	0.017	0.010	0.006

How to Build Wealth With Your 401(k)

Appendix A-3 Present Value of a Single Payment

Years	10%	12%	14%	15%	16%	18%	20%	25%	30%
1	0.909	0.893	0.877	0.870	0.862	0.847	0.833	0.800	0.769
2	0.826	0.797	0.769	0.756	0.743	0.718	0.694	0.640	0.592
3	0.751	0.712	0.675	0.658	0.641	0.609	0.579	0.512	0.455
4	0.683	0.636	0.592	0.572	0.552	0.516	0.482	0.410	0.350
5	0.621	0.567	0.519	0.497	0.476	0.437	0.402	0.328	0.269
6	0.564	0.507	0.456	0.432	0.410	0.370	0.335	0.262	0.207
7	0.513	0.452	0.400	0.376	0.354	0.314	0.279	0.210	0.159
8	0.467	0.404	0.351	0.327	0.305	0.266	0.233	0.168	0.123
9	0.424	0.361	0.308	0.284	0.263	0.225	0.194	0.134	0.094
10	0.386	0.322	0.270	0.247	0.227	0.191	0.162	0.107	0.073
11	0.350	0.287	0.237	0.215	0.195	0.162	0.135	0.086	0.056
12	0.319	0.257	0.208	0.187	0.168	0.137	0.112	0.069	0.043
13	0.290	0.229	0.182	0.163	0.145	0.116	0.093	0.055	0.033
14	0.263	0.205	0.160	0.141	0.125	0.099	0.078	0.044	0.025
15	0.239	0.183	0.140	0.123	0.108	0.084	0.065	0.035	0.020
16	0.218	0.163	0.123	0.107	0.093	0.071	0.054	0.028	0.015
17	0.198	0.146	0.108	0.093	0.080	0.060	0.045	0.023	0.012
18	0.180	0.130	0.095	0.081	0.069	0.051	0.038	0.018	0.009
19	0.164	0.116	0.083	0.070	0.060	0.043	0.031	0.014	0.007
20	0.149	0.104	0.073	0.061	0.051	0.037	0.026	0.012	0.005
21	0.135	0.093	0.064	0.053	0.044	0.031	0.022	0.009	0.004
22	0.123	0.083	0.056	0.046	0.038	0.026	0.018	0.007	0.003
23	0.112	0.074	0.049	0.040	0.033	0.022	0.015	0.006	0.002
24	0.102	0.066	0.043	0.035	0.028	0.019	0.013	0.005	0.002
25	0.092	0.059	0.038	0.030	0.024	0.016	0.010	0.004	0.001
26	0.084	0.053	0.033	0.026	0.021	0.014	0.009	0.003	0.001
27	0.076	0.047	0.029	0.023	0.018	0.011	0.007	0.002	0.001
28	0.069	0.042	0.026	0.020	0.016	0.010	0.006	0.002	0.001
29	0.063	0.037	0.022	0.017	0.014	0.008	0.005	0.002	0.000
30	0.057	0.033	0.020	0.015	0.012	0.007	0.004	0.001	0.000
31	0.052	0.030	0.017	0.013	0.010	0.006	0.004	0.001	0.000
32	0.047	0.027	0.015	0.011	0.009	0.005	0.003	0.001	0.000
33	0.043	0.024	0.013	0.010	0.007	0.004	0.002	0.001	0.000
34	0.039	0.021	0.012	0.009	0.006	0.004	0.002	0.001	0.000
35	0.036	0.019	0.010	0.008	0.006	0.003	0.002	0.000	0.000
40	0.022	0.011	0.005	0.004	0.003	0.001	0.001	0.000	0.000
45	0.014	0.006	0.003	0.002	0.001	0.001	0.000	0.000	0.000
50	0.009	0.003	0.001	0.001	0.001	0.000	0.000	0.000	0.000
55	0.005	0.002	0.001	0.000	0.000	0.000	0.000	0.000	0.000
60	0.003	0.001	0.000	0.000	0.000	0.000	0.000	0.000	0.000

Appendix A-4 Present Value of an Annuity

Years	1%	2%	3%	4%	5%	6%	7%	8%	9%
1	0.990	0.980	0.971	0.962	0.952	0.943	0.935	0.926	0.917
2	1.970	1.942	1.913	1.886	1.859	1.833	1.808	1.783	1.759
3	2.941	2.884	2.829	2.775	2.723	2.673	2.624	2.577	2.531
4	3.902	3.808	3.717	3.630	3.546	3.465	3.387	3.312	3.240
5	4.853	4.713	4.580	4.452	4.329	4.212	4.100	3.993	3.890
6	5.795	5.601	5.417	5.242	5.076	4.917	4.767	4.623	4.486
7	6.728	6.472	6.230	6.002	5.786	5.582	5.389	5.206	5.033
8	7.652	7.325	7.020	6.733	6.463	6.210	5.971	5.747	5.535
9	8.566	8.162	7.786	7.435	7.108	6.802	6.515	6.247	5.995
10	9.471	8.983	8.530	8.111	7.722	7.360	7.024	6.710	6.418
11	10.368	9.787	9.253	8.760	8.306	7.887	7.499	7.139	6.805
12	11.255	10.575	9.954	9.385	8.863	8.384	7.943	7.536	7.161
13	12.134	11.348	10.635	9.986	9.394	8.853	8.358	7.904	7.487
14	13.004	12.106	11.296	10.563	9.899	9.295	8.745	8.244	7.786
15	13.865	12.849	11.938	11.118	10.380	9.712	9.108	8.559	8.061
16	14.718	13.578	12.561	11.652	10.838	10.106	9.447	8.851	8.313
17	15.562	14.292	13.166	12.166	11.274	10.477	9.763	9.122	8.544
18	16.398	14.992	13.754	12.659	11.690	10.828	10.059	9.372	8.756
19	17.226	15.678	14.324	13.134	12.085	11.158	10.336	9.604	8.950
20	18.046	16.351	14.877	13.590	12.462	11.470	10.594	9.818	9.129
21	18.857	17.011	15.415	14.029	12.821	11.764	10.836	10.017	9.292
22	19.660	17.658	15.937	14.451	13.163	12.042	11.061	10.201	9.442
23	20.456	18.292	16.444	14.857	13.489	12.303	11.272	10.371	9.580
24	21.243	18.914	16.936	15.247	13.799	12.550	11.469	10.529	9.707
25	22.023	19.523	17.413	15.622	14.094	12.783	11.654	10.675	9.823
26	22.795	20.121	17.877	15.983	14.375	13.003	11.826	10.810	9.929
27	23.560	20.707	18.327	16.330	14.643	13.211	11.987	10.935	10.027
28	24.316	21.281	18.764	16.663	14.898	13.406	12.137	11.051	10.116
29	25.066	21.844	19.188	16.984	15.141	13.591	12.278	11.158	10.198
30	25.808	22.396	19.600	17.292	15.372	13.765	12.409	11.258	10.274
31	26.542	22.938	20.000	17.588	15.593	13.929	12.532	11.350	10.343
32	27.270	23.468	20.389	17.874	15.803	14.084	12.647	11.435	10.406
33	27.990	23.989	20.766	18.148	16.003	14.230	12.754	11.514	10.464
34	28.703	24.499	21.132	18.411	16.193	14.368	12.854	11.587	10.518
35	29.409	24.999	21.487	18.665	16.374	14.498	12.948	11.655	10.567
40	32.835	27.355	23.115	19.793	17.159	15.046	13.332	11.925	10.757
45	36.095	29.490	24.519	20.720	17.774	15.456	13.606	12.108	10.881
50	39.196	31.424	25.730	21.482	18.256	15.762	13.801	12.233	10.962
55	42.147	33.175	26.774	22.109	18.633	15.991	13.940	12.319	11.014
60	44.955	34.761	27.676	22.623	18.929	16.161	14.039	12.377	11.048

How to Build Wealth With Your 401(k)

Appendix A-4 Present Value of an Annuity

Years	10%	12%	14%	15%	16%	18%	20%	25%	30%
1	0.909	0.893	0.877	0.870	0.862	0.847	0.833	0.800	0.769
2	1.736	1.690	1.647	1.626	1.605	1.566	1.528	1.440	1.361
3	2.487	2.402	2.322	2.283	2.246	2.174	2.106	1.952	1.816
4	3.170	3.037	2.914	2.855	2.798	2.690	2.589	2.362	2.166
5	3.791	3.605	3.433	3.352	3.274	3.127	2.991	2.689	2.436
6	4.355	4.111	3.889	3.784	3.685	3.498	3.326	2.951	2.643
7	4.868	4.564	4.288	4.160	4.039	3.812	3.605	3.161	2.802
8	5.335	4.968	4.639	4.487	4.344	4.078	3.837	3.329	2.925
9	5.759	5.328	4.946	4.772	4.607	4.303	4.031	3.463	3.019
10	6.145	5.650	5.216	5.019	4.833	4.494	4.192	3.571	3.092
11	6.495	5.938	5.453	5.234	5.029	4.656	4.327	3.656	3.147
12	6.814	6.194	5.660	5.421	5.197	4.793	4.439	3.725	3.190
13	7.103	6.424	5.842	5.583	5.342	4.910	4.533	3.780	3.223
14	7.367	6.628	6.002	5.724	5.468	5.008	4.611	3.824	3.249
15	7.606	6.811	6.142	5.847	5.575	5.092	4.675	3.859	3.268
16	7.824	6.974	6.265	5.954	5.668	5.162	4.730	3.887	3.283
17	8.022	7.120	6.373	6.047	5.749	5.222	4.775	3.910	3.295
18	8.201	7.250	6.467	6.128	5.818	5.273	4.812	3.928	3.304
19	8.365	7.366	6.550	6.198	5.877	5.316	4.843	3.942	3.311
20	8.514	7.469	6.623	6.259	5.929	5.353	4.870	3.954	3.316
21	8.649	7.562	6.687	6.312	5.973	5.384	4.891	3.963	3.320
22	8.772	7.645	6.743	6.359	6.011	5.410	4.909	3.970	3.323
23	8.883	7.718	6.792	6.399	6.044	5.432	4.925	3.976	3.325
24	8.985	7.784	6.835	6.434	6.073	5.451	4.937	3.981	3.327
25	9.077	7.843	6.873	6.464	6.097	5.467	4.948	3.985	3.329
26	9.161	7.896	6.906	6.491	6.118	5.480	4.956	3.988	3.330
27	9.237	7.943	6.935	6.514	6.136	5.492	4.964	3.990	3.331
28	9.307	7.984	6.961	6.534	6.152	5.502	4.970	3.992	3.331
29	9.370	8.022	6.983	6.551	6.166	5.510	4.975	3.994	3.332
30	9.427	8.055	7.003	6.566	6.177	5.517	4.979	3.995	3.332
31	9.479	8.085	7.020	6.579	6.187	5.523	4.982	3.996	3.332
32	9.526	8.112	7.035	6.591	6.196	5.528	4.985	3.997	3.333
33	9.569	8.135	7.048	6.600	6.203	5.532	4.988	3.997	3.333
34	9.609	8.157	7.060	6.609	6.210	5.536	4.990	3.998	3.333
35	9.644	8.176	7.070	6.617	6.215	5.539	4.992	3.998	3.333
40	9.779	8.244	7.105	6.642	6.233	5.548	4.997	3.999	3.333
45	9.863	8.283	7.123	6.654	6.242	5.552	4.999	4.000	3.333
50	9.915	8.304	7.133	6.661	6.246	5.554	4.999	4.000	3.333
55	9.947	8.317	7.138	6.664	6.248	5.555	5.000	4.000	3.333
60	9.967	8.324	7.140	6.665	6.249	5.555	5.000	4.000	3.333

APPENDIX B

Information Sources

Information Sources

National Association of 401(k) Investors

The National Association of 401(k) Investors (NA4I) is a nonprofit organization that teaches people how to invest in their 401(k) plans. Beginning and experienced investors are invited to join, as are people who have similar retirement plans such as a 403(b), 457, Thrift Savings Plan for federal employees, SIMPLE, and SAR-SEP plan.

Members receive a one-year subscription to the *401(k) Journal*, unlimited use of a Q&A Infoline and either a free copy of this book (valued at $19.95) or two free reports, "What to Do With Your Retirement Account When You Leave the Company" and "All About Self-Directed IRA Investing" (a total value of $24.00). You also get discounts on other information sources including a professionally prepared analysis of your own 401(k) investments. Membership dues are $39 per year.

NA4I is an educational organization. No other organization controls or directs its activities and they accept no advertising or endorsement revenues from any outside sources. By remaining independent of any company engaged in the sale of financial products NA4I is able to provide an unbiased approach to educating 401(k) investors. I highly recommend this organization. For more information, call **(407) 636-5737**. To join, send a check or money order for $39 to **National Association of 401(k) Investors, Membership Services, P.O. Box 410755, Melbourne, FL 32941**. Be sure to indicate whether you want a copy of this book or the two information reports as part of your membership.

Government Information

Social Security

The Social Security Administration provides many informative pamphlets at no cost. You can obtain free information by calling 1-800-772-1213. The hours of operation are 7 A.M. to 7 P.M. You can request an earnings and benefit estimate statement showing the earnings and credits currently applied toward your future Social Security benefits. Use the 1-800 number and ask for form SSA-7004.

Recommended Government Publications

- A Guide to Social Security Retirement Benefits; Pub 05-10035.
- Understanding Social Security; Pub 05-10024.
- A Guide to the Medicare Program; Pub 05-10043.

Tax Information from the Internal Revenue Service

The IRS has many publications covering tax laws. They can be ordered by calling 1-800-829-3676. Publication 910 is a list of all available publications.

Most libraries carry tax publications and tax information including the Internal Revenue Code (IRC). Good luck trying to make heads or tails of this publication. It is no wonder we have thousands of tax lawyers and spend millions in courts each year trying to interpret the tax codes.

Consumer Information

The U.S. General Services Administration (GSA) operates a consumer information service. You can get a catalog of low-cost federal publications of general interest to consumers. Most publications are either free or less than $1 each. Keep in mind that these publications are government managed so you get what you pay for!

To get the catalog, write to the following address:

Consumer Information Center - 4A
P.O. Box 100
Pueblo, Colorado 81002

Recommended Publications

- Looking Out for # 2: A married couple's guide to understanding your benefit choices at retirement from a *defined
  contribution plan.* Publication 1565 (12-91); Catalog
  Number 13095T.

- Looking Out for # 2. A married couple's guide to understanding your benefit choices at retirement from a *defined
  benefit plan.* Publication 1566 (12-91). Catalog Number
  13096E.

Retirement Associations

The American Association of Retired Persons (AARP) is for
Americans over 50 years of age, but you don't have to be
retired to join. Membership is only $8 per year and gives you
access to many good resources.

American Association of Retired Persons (AARP)
601 E Street, NW
Washington, DC 20049

Stock and Bond Information

The following three resources carry good information for those
who invest in individual securities. They can be found in the
reference section of most libraries.

Moody's Investors Services
99 Church Street,
N.Y., N.Y. 10007
212-553-0547

Standard & Poor's
25 Broadway,
N.Y., N.Y. 10004
1-800-221-7940

Value Line
Stock Survey
220 East 42nd Street
New York, N.Y. 10017-5891
1-800-833-0046

Mutual Fund and Stock Market Analysis Information

The following three companies offer good information on mutual funds, but the cost is prohibitive for most individual investors. A good alternative is to check out the reference section of your local library.

Morningstar Mutual Funds
225 West Wacker Drive,
Chicago, Illinois 60606
1-800-876-5005

Value Line
Mutual Fund Survey
220 East 42nd Street
New York, NY 10017-5891
1-800-833-0046

CDA / Wiesenberger Mutual Fund Update
1355 Piccard Drive,
Rockville, MD 20850
1-800-232-2285

The following three books carry good information. They are designed for individuals investing in low- or no-load funds.

The Mutual Fund Encyclopedia
680 N. Lake Shore Drive
Tower Offices #2038
Chicago, IL 60611
1-800-326-6941

The Handbook for No-Load Fund Investors
P.O. Box 283
Hastings-on-Hudson, N.Y. 10706
914-693-7420

The Individual Investor's Guide to Low-Load Mutual Fund
American Association of Individual Investors
625 N. Michigan Avenue,
Suite 1900,
Chicago, IL. 60611
312-280-0170

Newspapers

Newspapers are the most popular source of information for market indexes and mutual fund category performances. The Wall Street Journal has a year-end issue that covers many market indexes and mutual fund category performances. It also has detailed information on other investment subjects but a subscription is not generally cost effective for most 401(k) investors. Once again, your local library may be able to help.

- Wall Street Journal; Dow Jones Publisher
- Investor's Business Daily
- Barron's; Dow Jones Publisher
- Local papers. Most daily papers list market indexes, along with individual returns for stocks and mutual funds.

Magazines

The following list contains just a few of the many investment magazines available. Forbes and Financial World are geared more toward experienced investors. Money and Kiplinger's target the novice investor. Each magazine offers good information hidden between pages of advertising. I recommend Kiplinger's. It is inexpensive, informative and well written.

- Forbes
- Money
- Kiplinger's
- Worth
- Financial World
- Smart Money
- Individual Investor

APPENDIX C

Variable Annuity Contracts

Variable Annuity Contracts

If your 401(k) or 403(b) plan is set up as a variable annuity, then you will need to read the information in this appendix carefully. A variable annuity is very common in 403(b) plans and not so common in 401(k) plans. This arrangement has some very big disadvantages. It contains excessive hidden charges that can severely degrade the performance of your investments.

A variable annuity is a special arrangement created by an insurance company for your employer. It is basically a set of mutual funds enclosed within an insurance wrapper. See Figure C-1. The mutual funds are referred to as separate accounts. There is typically an equity, bond and money market account to choose from. Only individuals participating in the annuity contract can invest in these funds.

The separate accounts within the arrangement are just like any other mutual fund. Their performance can be good, average or poor. The insurance contract is what makes the arrangement different. The contract guarantees your principle investment upon your death. This means if you have invested $100,000 and your account value is $80,000 when you die, then your beneficiary will receive $100,000. This assumes you did not withdraw any of the $100,0000 principle prior to your death. If your account value is worth $200,000, you receive the $200,000 value of your account. This death benefit is not free. It will cost you about 1.5 percent of your account value each year and is paid to the insurance company. This amount directly reduces your return.

Not only do you pay for the death benefit, but variable annuity contracts have many other hidden charges in addition to normal fund expenses. Total charges can run as high as 2 percent, depending on the insurance company, but 1.5 percent is more common. This expense contributes no added value to the growth of your investment.

Figure C-1   Variable Annuity Arrangement

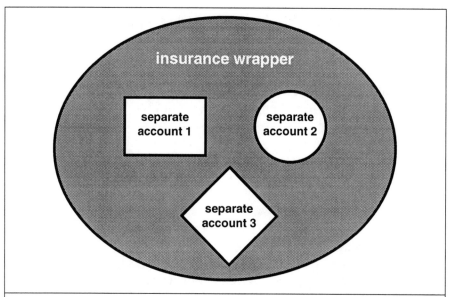

This is a graphical representation of a variable annuity arrangement. It shows that a variable annuity arrangement is made of several separate accounts surrounded by an insurance wrapper. The separate accounts are mutual funds that are only available to investors who participate in the variable annuity contract.

How Contract Expenses Impact Your Investment

Let's take a look at how the expense is applied to your account. If a fund within the annuity arrangement returns 10 percent and variable annuity expenses are 2 percent, then the actual return on your account is less than 8 percent. Likewise, if the fund drops 4 percent, the return on your separate account drops by more than 6 percent. Yes, they collect their fee in good times and bad! It is important to note that the 2 percent contract charge is typically applied to the entire balance of your funds and not just the investment return.

When evaluating the performance of separate accounts be sure to take into account expenses associated with the insurance contract. You will often find that performance history quotes do not include expenses. For example, annual reports usually show performance of the mutual fund before contract expenses are subtracted. If you read the small print you will see that expenses and other product charges are not reflected in the data.

Be sure to find out fund performance both before and after expenses. By comparing fund performance before expenses to the appropriate benchmark you can find out how good the fund is. But to find out your true return, you will need to subtract out the percentage of expenses charged to your account.

As an example, let's compare actual performance numbers between two S&P 500 index funds. The first fund is outside an annuity contract and the second is inside. Both funds have the same objective to track the S&P 500. We'll use the Vanguard Index 500 fund for the fund outside the contract. It is a popular, no-load mutual fund available to all investors. Table C-1 shows one and five year returns for the Vanguard fund, the separate account before expenses, and the separate account after expenses. You will see that their returns are very similar until you look at the separate account after expenses.

Table C-1   Variable Annuity Arrangement

	1993	5 Year Average
S&P 500 Index	10.06	14.52
Vanguard Index 500 Mutual Fund	9.89	14.31
Separate Account Before Expenses	9.7	14
Separate Account After Expenses	8.09	12.4
Lehman Brothers Bond Aggregate Index	9.75	11.25

This table shows how the expenses associated with a variable annuity can drastically reduce your investment return. The Vanguard fund is a fund outside the annuity contract. It's objective is to mirror the S&P 500 index. You can see that Vanguard's one and five year performances meet it's objective. The separate account is a fund available within an annuity contract. It's objective is also to mirror the S&P 500, which it does until you look at it's return after expenses. The real return of the separate account is approximately 2 percent below the index it's supposed to track. You can also see that it doesn't do much better than the bond index which has a much lower risk.

Both the Vanguard fund and the separate account before expenses returned slightly less than the S&P 500 index. This slight reduction is due to normal fund management expenses. The return for the separate account after expenses, however, is a different story. Notice that annuity expenses drag the separate account's performance significantly lower than the S&P 500 benchmark (which it is supposed to track) and significantly lower than the Vanguard fund. This is especially true when the period is extended to five years. Over five years you can see that the separate account's performance is reduced from 14 percent to 12.4 percent. This reduction can certainly impede wealth building!

Are the Expenses Worth The Principle Guarantee?

OK, so variable annuity expenses are a big drag on the growth of your investment. The question now is whether or not the charges are worth the death benefit guarantee. When trying to build wealth for retirement the answer is an easy "no way". The reasons are simple.

First, you should already have the proper life insurance coverage needed to protect your loved ones, i.e. term insurance though a group policy, so you do not need additional expensive insurance. Second, your account value will likely grow over time and significantly exceed your principle investment. Of course there may be times when your account value is less than the principle you invested, but in the long run this is not likely to happen. The exception to this is if you are invested in a separate account so bad that you can't make any money. In this case the variable annuity let you down.

Paying an insurance premium for the guarantee of principle is a lousy return on your investment. To impede growth of your investment by 2 percent in order to guarantee the principle upon your death does not make sense when trying to build wealth. A difference of 2 percent over twenty or thirty years makes an incredible difference to the final value of your account. Take a look at your future value tables and see for yourself!

Not all 403(b) plans use the variable annuity contract. Some are set up with no-load mutual fund companies instead of variable annuity contracts so there is no additional expenses associated with an insurance wrapper.

Should You Invest In a 403(b) or 401(k) with a Variable Annuity?

The question remaining to be answered is whether or not it is worth investing in a 403(b) or 401(k) plan that is arranged as a variable annuity contract. Although the annuity contract by itself is a poor investment, the addition of the 403(b) or 401(k) provides you with the opportunity for double tax deferment. You may remember that contributions to a 403(b) or 401(k) are tax deferred and that the interest your account earns is also tax deferred.

The question, therefore, is whether or not it is worth paying the annuity contract expense that adds no value to your investment in exchange for the privilege of tax deferral. If you are eligible for tax deductible contributions to an Individual Retirement Account (IRA), then you have at your disposal a tax-deferred investment that doesn't have the added annuity contract expense. Use this investment to your advantage first. Even if you aren't eligible for tax-deferred IRA contributions, an IRA still allows your investment to grow tax-deferred. Whether or not you should invest in a variable annuity arrangement if you are not eligible for tax-deferred IRA contributions is a tough question. It depends largely on your situation so you need to explore all your investment options. If you do decide to invest in the annuity contract, be sure to emphasize growth funds so that the higher returns will potentially overcome the annuity fees. Its also important to investigate the fee structure and analyze the separate accounts inside the contract.

IRA Investing; A Good Alternative

A self-directed IRA allows you to invest in top performing, no-load mutual funds without the excessive fees that come with your variable annuity contract. You also have an almost unlimited number of funds to choose from. You are not limited to the two or three options found within your annuity contract.

If your adjusted gross income is below $40,000 for a married couple filing jointly, or below $25,000 for a single filer you are eligible for up to a $2,000 tax deductible contribution into an individual IRA or $2,250 for a spousal IRA. If both you and your spouse work and each has at least $2,000 of earned income, then you both are eligible for an IRA contribution of $2,000 each for a total of $4,000. You are eligible for a partial contribution if your earnings are above those stated and below the cut off limits of $50,000 for married filers and $35,000 for single filers.

If your 401(k) or 403(b) offers matching funds, then you should contribute up to the matching amount before turning to the IRA. Any additional non-matching contributions can then be made into an IRA. By contributing up to the matching amount, you will lower your Adjusted Gross Income (AGI) and possibly become eligible for tax deductible IRA contributions if you weren't already.

If your plan does not offer a match, then you should consider investing first in an IRA then any other additional contributions can be made to the annuity. A non-matching variable annuity is very common in 403(b) plans so you may want to invest in an IRA first. This strategy allows you to build up a good IRA account while you are still eligible for tax deductible IRA contributions. As your salary increases, you can contribute to the annuity to take advantage of tax deferral and perhaps lower your AGI in order to continue your tax deductible IRA eligibility.

Real-Life Choices that Can Add One Million Dollars to Your Final Account Value

John and Mary, a married couple, are both 25 and just starting to save for retirement. John earns $30,000 a year as a high school teacher. He has the opportunity to contribute to a non-matching 403(b) plan. Mary earns about $5,000 a year from part-time work. John and Mary are eligible to make tax-deferred contributions to an IRA. They can contribute $2,000 each into their own IRA's since they both have earned income. Contributing $2,000 each allows them a total of $4,000 in tax deferred contributions.

John and Mary want to take advantage of self-directed IRA investing since John's 403(b) does not offer matching contributions. They decide they can afford to contribute $3,000 total for the year. Their plan is to contribute $125 a month into a self-directed IRA for John and another $125 into an IRA for Mary. Their IRA's will be set up directly with a top-performing no-load mutual fund company. Since they are new to investing they decide to invest in an S&P 500 index fund.

By avoiding the 403(b) annuity contract, John and Mary have an extra 2 percent return working for them for the next 40 years. Based on past performance of the S&P 500, the additional 2 percent will add $975,000 to their final account value! This is almost one million dollars more than if they had invested in an expensive separate account with the same investment risk and return! By making this one simple investment decision, John and Mary are able to drastically improve the quality of their life. As you can see, a little knowledge can go a long way! Let's look at another example.

Bill and Sally are both employed by an elementary school. The school offers a 403(b) plan that will match 50 cents on the dollar up to the first $2,500 of contributions made. Their combined salary leaves them with an AGI of $50,000. At this AGI level they are not eligible for tax deductible contributions to an IRA so they decide to contribute to $2,500 each into their 403(b) plan in order to receive all the matching funds. Their

Figure C-2 Variable Annuity Arrangement

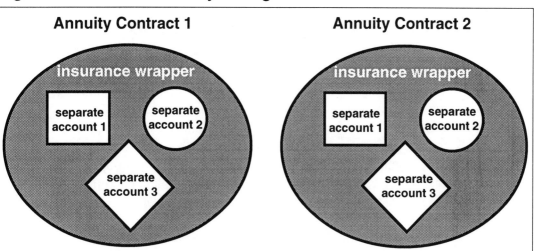

This is a graphical representation of a variable annuity arrangement where two different insurance contracts are available. If you invest in both contracts, you will likely have to pay two custodial fees; one for each contract.

total contribution of $5,000 into the 403(b) lowers their AGI to $45,000. This now makes them each eligible for a $1,000 tax deductible IRA contribution.

Bill and Sally's total tax deferred income is now $7,000 because they invested $5,000 into their 403(b) and an additional $2,000 into two IRA's. Don't forget they also get $2,500 in matching funds from their employer so they now have a total of $9,500 invested in retirement accounts.

If you desire to build wealth you may be forced to take a bigger risk for less return in a variable annuity. Concentrate your separate account selections in growth equity funds so that you can do your best to overcome the 2 percent expense. If your accounts end up losing money you will at least get your principle back when you die!

Your Employer May Have More Than One Annuity Contract

Many 403(b) plans offer several different annuity contracts. See Figure C-2. Each annuity will have different separate accounts to choose from. Be sure to evaluate each annuity contract as we have discussed and select the best ones in which to invest. Each contract will likely have different expenses so be sure to include this in your analysis. The goal is to choose the contract with the best performing separate accounts and with the lowest contract fees.

There is usually a fixed custodial account fee that goes along with each annuity contract. The fee runs from $30 to $100. This is in addition to the other fees we have already talked about. If you are just getting started with your retirement investments it does not pay to be in more than one annuity contract because of the fixed fee expense. Pick the annuity contract with the best separate accounts that satisfy your objectives.

Is Your 403(b) Set Up as a Variable Annuity?

The biggest user of 403(b) plans are public schools. Most use variable annuity contracts set up by major insurance companies. These plans are often established with three or four different annuity contracts to choose from. Employers do not have to arrange their 403(b) plans as a variable annuity. An arrangement can be made that is similar to a self directed IRA. You may want to talk to your benefits administrator about setting up your 403(b) plan with one of the leading no-load mutual fund companies.

No-load fund companies like Twentieth Century, Janus, and Vanguard offer 403(b) accounts that are not variable annuities. This allows you to invest in some of the best mutual funds available without the expensive annuity contract impeding you ability to build wealth. Fidelity Investments offers many excellent no-load funds available through retirement plans. If your employer is willing to improve their 403(b) or 401(k) plan but needs help, they can contact the National Association of 401(k) Investors by writing to the following address: **National Association of 401(k) Investors, P.O. Box 410755, Melbourne, FL 32941. Their phone number is (407) 636-5737**.

Glossary

401(k) plan   A special defined contribution plan that allows for employees to defer salary compensation on a pre-tax basis. 401(k) is the section of the Internal Revenue Code that permits this type of plan.

403(b) plan   Section 403(b) of the Internal Revenue Code (IRC) allows qualified non-profit organizations to establish a tax qualified plan for employees.

457 plan   Section 457 of Internal revenue code that allows municipal and state government organizations to establish a qualified tax deferred plan for employees.

asset allocation   The process of distributing portfolio investments across different asset classes such as stocks, bonds, and cash equivalents.

asset class   An asset class categorizes similar types of investments. Stocks make up an asset class, while bonds make of a different asset class. A portfolio made up of stocks and bonds would be investing in two different asset classes.

bear market   Term used to describe a period of pessimism and declining returns in the stock market.

benchmarking   The process of comparing the output of an event against a known standard.

beneficiary   A person eligible to receive the benefits of a participant if the participant dies.

bull market   Term used to describe optimism and general increase in returns of the stock market.

business risk   A non systematic risk associated with the unique aspects of a particular business.

capital appreciation   The increase in market value of an investment above the purchase price.

capital gain   The realization of capital appreciation when an investment is sold.

capital loss   The realization of a decrease in market value of an investment when sold.

capital market   Financial market used to trade long term debt and equities.

cash equivalents   Debt securities with a maturity of less than one year. The short maturity length makes the debt very liquid and it's value stable.

CODA   Cash or Deferred Arrangement. An accounting term used to describe the type of plans such as a 401(k) which allow the employee the option receiving their salary in cash or deferring it in an investment plan.

commingled IRA account   An IRA that contains money rolled over from a qualified company retirement plan and money contributed by the IRA owner separate from a qualified company retirement plan.

common stocks   The basic form of ownership of a corporation.

conduit IRA   An IRA that contains only moneys associated with a rollover from a qualified company retirement plan.

Consumer Price Index (CPI)   A government statistical measure designed to provide a means of estimating inflation.

credit rating   The rating associated with a issuer of debt instruments ability to make payments on the instrument. The credit rating may very positive or negative over the length of the debts maturity depending on the issuers health.

credit risk   The non systematic risk associated with the ability of a issuer of debt to fulfill the payment of the debt.

currency risk   Non systematic risk associated with the constant variation in different currencies value in relationship to each other. The value of foreign stock is influenced by the strength or weakness of the currency in which it is held.

current income   The periodic cash distribution from an investment.

defined benefit plan   A retirement plan that pays a known benefit at retirement. This type of plan is the traditional company pension.

defined contribution plan   A retirement plan that final value is based on the contributions to the plan and the investment performance. The 401(k) ESOP, and profit sharing plan are popular defined contribution plans.

direct rollover   When the new plan trustee receives your money directly from the original agent.

diversification   The portfolio strategy of spreading your investments across different companies and industries to avoid any upset in a particular industry or company.

DJIA   Dow Jones industrial Average is a market index that uses 30 large industrial stocks to gauge the stock market. The DJIA is considered an index that represents the movement of blue chip stocks.

dollar cost averaging   See systematic investing

DOL   Department of Labor

efficient market   The modern portfolio theory that states all information about a particular investment is quickly

known by investors and immediately reflected in the securities value.

equities   Stocks are referred to as equities since a stock share holder is entitled to the equity in the company.

ERISA   Employee Retirement Income Securities Act. Federal Act established to set rules and regulations to protect employees who are participants in company retirement plans. The department of labor is responsible for the regulation of company retirement plans and the enforcement of ERISA.

ESOP   Employee Stock Ownership Program. A defined contribution plan that invest primarily in employers company stock.

fiduciary   A person who has authority or control over the management of money.

financial planning   The planning of all aspects of an individuals finances.

fixed annuity   A contract that provides a known payment for a specified period of time independent of investment results.

foreign fund   A fund that invest entirely in foreign (no U.S) securities. It may invest in a particular country, region, or a wide range of countries.

future value   The future value of an investment earning compound interest over some period of time.

geometric mean   Statistical averaging method used to calculate average returns of compounding interest.

global fund   A fund that may invest in both foreign and US securities.

Guaranteed Investment Contracts   An insurance company product that offers a fixed rate of return for a defined period. Available to institutional investors.

hardship withdrawal   A method of withdrawing funds from a 401(k) plan prior to retirement. It requires a proven hardship.

index fund A fund that invest in the same stocks as a particular index. The S&P 500 stock index is a popular index that is replicated by index funds.

inflation The increase in overall cost of goods and services. Inflation drives the prices of consumer goods up and decreases the dollars purchasing power.

inflation risk The systematic risk that erodes away the value of money over time.

institutional fund Mutual fund available through pension funds. Institutional funds are not available directly to individual investors.

investment grade The highest most favorable category of bond credit risk rating. It represents the bonds whose issuers have the best opportunity to make payments.

IRA Individual Retirement Account. A tax deferral retirement investment plan permitted by the IRS for individuals who have earned income. The individual is responsible for setting up and contributing to the plan.

IRC Internal Revenue Code. The federal document that defines the US tax system.

IRS Internal Revenue Service. Government agency tasked with enforcing the rules and collection of the internal revenue code.

junk bond The lowest least favorable category of bond credit risk rating. It identifies the bonds whose issuers have the minimal opportunity to repay the debt.

Keogh plan A qualified tax deferred plan designed for the self-employed.

liquidity The speed and ease with which an asset can be converted to cash.

lump sum distribution The receiving of one's entire qualified retirement plan from an employer.

market capitalization The total market value of a companies outstanding stock. It is determined by multiply the market price of a single share of a companies stock by the total number of outstanding shares.

market correction A term used to describe a set back in the stock markets gain. This is also known as a bear market.

market indexes Statistical measures of performance designed to gauge the performance of the overall stock market or some specific portion of the market.

market risk The systematic risk that the markets as a whole will perform poorly.

money market fund A fund that invest entirely in cash equivalents. The fund may be taxable or tax exempt.

mutual fund Investment money pooled together by individual investors and managed by a professional fund manager.

NASDAQ Composite A market index that is made up of predominately small stocks traded on NASDAQ. It is considered the best index for small stocks.

net asset value (NAV) The net asset value is the daily valuation of a mutual funds investment value. It is the calculate by computing the market closing value of all securities in the fund then subtracting out expenses. The net value is then divided by the number of mutual funds shares. This results in a NAV for the fund.

principal The amount of initial money or subsequent money invested in a investment.

probate   A court procedure for settling and disposing of an estate.

profit sharing plan   A contribution plan where employers make contributions on behalf of the employees to an account set of for the employee.

prospectus   A document required by the SEC that contains certain information pertaining to an investment that is being offered to the public

qualified retirement plan   a retirement plan that is structured under IRS guidelines and qualifies for special tax treatment.

real return   The real return of an investment is the actual return percentage less the inflation rate. This results in an investors real rate of return over inflation affects.

retail fund   Mutual fund sold to individuals either directly or through a broker.

retirement plan   An investment vehicle that has favorable advantages for retirement investing. The plan may be a IRA qualified or non qualified plan.

risk   Risk from an investment standpoint is the possibility that an investment may be worth less after some time period.

rollover   The process of moving funds from one qualified retirement account to another without losing tax deferral.

rollover paid to you   When your account is liquidated and the money is sent to you less 20 percent which is withheld for income taxes.

S&P 500 Index   A market index calculated by Standard and Poor's that uses 500 stocks in a statistical measure of the entire stock market.

SEC   Securities and Exchange Commission. Tasked with regulating the investment industry.

SEP   Simplified Employee Pension. A qualified retirement plan for small business and self employed. The plan has simplified administrative requirements which makes it attractive to small employers.

SIMPLE   Saving Incentive Match Plan for Employees. New retirement plan designated for companies with fewer than 100 employees. It is designed to simplify paper work and requirements for small businesses.

Summary Plan Description   Company retirement plan description which includes employee rights as required by ERISA.

systematic investing   The process of investing on a continuous basis regardless of the financial market performance. This will allow an investor to purchase more shares when the markets are down and less shares when the markets are high. This will typically produce a lower average price per share.

systematic risk   Uniform risk that is common to all investors. This includes market risk, inflation, and credit risk.

tax-advantaged   A tax-advantage investment is one where an investments gains are either deferred or exempt thereby producing an investment advantage to the investor.

tax-deferred   A tax deferred investment is one where the investment gains are not taxed in the year they are made, but deferred to some future time. This is usually retirement, and taxes are due when money is withdrawn.

tax-exempt   A tax exempt investment is one where the interest return is not subject to federal and possibly state or local taxes.

tax free rollover   A method in which a lump sum distribution is rolled over to another qualified plan continuing tax deferment of the investment money.

thrift savings plan The federal government has established a special thrift savings plan for civil employees. The plan operates as a defined contribution plan.

total return Dividends, interest, or other income received from an investment plus or minus capital appreciation or depreciation.

Treasury Bill A short term debt obligation issued by the US. Treasury having a maturity of less than one year. Also referred to as T-Bills.

Treasury Bond A bond issued by the US treasury that has a maturity of 10 years or more. The bonds are issued to finance the US governments operations.

Treasury Notes Treasury notes are similar to the bonds but have a maturity length of two to 5 years.

trustee A person or agency who is responsible for the handling of an individual or organizations assets.

unsystematic risk Non uniform risk that is associated with a particular company or industry.

vesting ERISA rule that requires employer contributions to become a nonforfeitable right to employees after a certain time frame. Vesting is usually based on a five year cliff or seven year gradual schedule.

yield The percentage of return of a securities dividend or interest in relation to the securities current value. A $10 security that has a $1 dividend payout per year has a yield of 10 percent.

How to Build Wealth With Your 401(k)

Index

present value 44
  annuity 45
  single payment 44
profit sharing plan 10

Q

qualified account 140

R

responsibility of employee 11, 13
responsibility of employer 13, 22, 24
restrictions 138
risk 55
  bonds 71
  company 57, 71, 72
  industry 57
  inflation 56, 71
  interest rate 56, 71
  market 56
  reducing 58, 151
  stocks 64
  systematic 56, 67, 71
  trade-off 57, 152
  unsystematic 57, 67
rollover 21, 140
  direct rollover 140
  into another 401(k) 142
  rollover paid to you 141

S

S&P 500 64
salary deferred plans 11
  401(k) 10
  403(b) 12
  457 12
  Thrift Savings Plan 13
SAR-SEP 136
shareholder 60
SIMPLE 136

small business retirement plans 13
Social Security 7
  Social Security Act of 1935 7
speculating 151
stock classification 63
stockholder 60
stocks 60
  blue chip 63
  common stocks 60
  cyclical 64
  growth 63
  historical returns 84
  in your portfolio 75
  income 63
  large caps 63
  mid caps 62
  preferred stocks 61
  risk 64
  small caps 62
  speculative 64
Summary Plan Description 23, 25
systematic investing 100, 151

T

tax deferment 15, 149
tax avoidance 149
ten-year averaging 145
Thrift Savings Plan 13, 26, 136, 145
time horizon 150
Treasury Bill 84, 94

V

variable annuity 135, 143, 170
vesting 24, 138

W

withdrawals 20
worksheets 27, 118

Information Reports by Steve Merritt

- What to Do With Your Retirement Account
  When You Leave the Company......................$12

- All About Self-Directed IRA Investing.........$12

- All About Variable Annuity Investing...........$12

- Street Smart Investing; A behind-the-scenes look
  at sales tactics used in the industry................$10

To order, send check or money order along with your request to **Halyard Press, Inc., Orders Dept., P.O. Box 410308, Melbourne, FL 32941**. Shipping and handling is <u>free</u>. Please add 6 percent for reports shipped to Florida addresses.

About the National Association of 401(k) Investors

The National Association of 401(k) Investors is a nonprofit, public education organization that teaches people how to invest in 401(k) and similar retirement plans. Membership is $39 per year and includes a one-year subscription to the *401(k) Journal,* unlimited use of the Q&A Infoline, and either a free copy of this book (valued at $19.95) or two free reports, "What to Do With Your Retirement Account When You Leave the Company" and "All About Self-Directed IRA Investing" (a total value of $24.00). You also get discounts on other information sources including a professionally prepared analysis of your own 401(k) investments. For more information, call **(407) 636-5737**. To join, send a check or money order for $39 to **National Association of 401(k) Investors, Membership Services, P.O. Box 410755, Melbourne, FL 32941.** Be sure to indicate whether you want a copy of this book or the two information reports with your membership.